CW00520839

A handbook
for presentation skills

GARY KROEHNERT

McGRAW-HILL BOOK COMPANY Sydney
New York San Francisco Auckland Bangkok Bogota Caracas
Hong Kong Kuala Lumpur Lisbon London Madrid Mexico City Milan Montreal
New Delhi San Juan Seoul Singapore Taipei Toronto

McGraw·Hill Australia

A Division of The **McGraw·Hill** *Companies*

Reprinted 1999
Text © 1998 Gary Kroehnert
Illustrations and design © 1998 McGraw-Hill Book Company Australia Pty Limited
Additional owners of copyright are named in on-page credits.

Apart from any fair dealing for the purposes of study, research, criticism or review, as permitted under the *Copyright Act*, no part may be reproduced by any process without written permission. Enquiries should be made to the publisher, marked for the attention of the Permissions Editor, at the address below.

Every effort has been made to trace and acknowledge copyright material. Should any infringement have occurred accidentally the authors and publishers tender their apologies.

Copying for educational purposes
Under the copying provisions of the *Copyright Act*, copies of parts of this book may be made by an educational institution. An agreement exists between the Copyright Agency Limited (CAL) and the relevant educational authority (Department of Education, university, TAFE, etc.) to pay a licence fee for such copying. It is not necessary to keep records of copying except where the relevant educational authority has undertaken to do so by arrangement with the Copyright Agency Limited.

For further information on the CAL licence agreements with educational institutions, contact the Copyright Agency Limited, Level 19, 157 Liverpool Street, Sydney NSW 2000. Where no such agreement exists, the copyright owner is entitled to claim payment in respect of any copies made.

Enquiries concerning copyright in McGraw-Hill publications should be directed to the Permissions Editor at the address below.

National Library of Australia Cataloguing-in-Publication data:

    Kroehnert, Gary.
      Basic presentation skills.

      Includes index.
      ISBN 0 07 470606 3.

      1. Business presentations. I. Title.

658.452

Published in Australia by
McGraw-Hill Book Company Australia Pty Limited
4 Barcoo Street, Roseville NSW 2069, Australia

Acquisitions Editors: John Rowe, Kristen Baragwanath
Supervising Editor: Sybil Kesteven
Editor: Carolyn Pike
Cover design: Loui Silvestro
Cartoonist: Loui Silvestro
Technical illustrator: Lorenzo Lucia, Tech View Studio
Typeset by Wordsworth Marketing Services
Printed by Hillwing Printing Co. Hong Kong

Contents

Preface

(Please read it!)

In my first training book titled *Basic Training for Trainers* I said that in many ways the design, presentation and evaluation of a course is like the preparation of a meal. A meal is not simply the collection of various foods which are thrown into a pot to cook. The ingredients have to be selected according to the recipe, they have to be prepared, and they have to be cooked individually, perhaps using different methods and having other ingredients added to them in the correct sequence while they are cooking.

If the various elements are collected, prepared and organised properly we will have a professional looking presentation. If the presentation looks good, we have the best chance of it being taken without resistance. If the course is taken, enjoyed and sustains life or develops growth, isn't it possible that we have taken care of the evaluation as well? I haven't changed my thoughts on this; in fact they have been really reinforced over the past few years. This book on presentation skills includes all of the same ingredients as *Basic Training for Trainers*, though some are slightly modified.

As with the first and second editions of *Basic Training for Trainers* it is not intended that this book be a complete resource in itself. It is again intended that this book be written in simple, easy-to-understand terms. It should become part of a simple resource kit for the public speaker, presenter or student. It is meant to give new presenters an overview of the main competencies they will need to develop skills in.

Many people have different ideas about what 'presentation skills' really means. What we are looking at in this book is the set of skills a person needs to offer both effective information presentations and effective training presentations, and what skills are needed to be an effective public speaker. These presentations are generally linked in with some kind of learning or information sharing.

As a result some chapters will be more relevant than others. For example, it may be that some people reading this handbook know that they will be giving presentations to groups of people as a training course. Therefore, Chapter One on 'The principles of adult learning and retention' will be extremely relevant for them. On the other hand someone might be reading this handook knowing that they will be asked to organise the staff Christmas party and be the MC. In this case Chapter One may not be relevant at all!

While this book looks mainly at the learning type of presentation, the skills and techniques shown also apply to the standard type of information presentation for the public speaker. Regardless of which terms are used—trainer, presenter, instructor, facilitator or public speaker—they all mean basically the same thing. And that is to pass information on to other people. Likewise the terms audience, participant, student and learner all have similar meanings. And that is to gain information, whether for learning, fun or entertainment. The point here is, don't get hung up on the terms, but rather look at the content and see how it can relate to your needs.

This book has been formatted at the request of my previous readers to allow plenty of room around the margins to make relevant notes as you go through. Read actively with a pen in hand and take advantage of this!

Most chapters in this book have their own application example and a list of resources for further reading. I have not included texts which were found to be too awkward for the newcomer. If you would like to suggest other inclusions please fill in the form found at the back of this text with your suggestions. This form may also be used for comments on layout, spelling, or anything you wish. These suggestions will be evaluated for inclusion in further editions.

After you have read this text, it is hoped that it will be kept as a quick reference guide. Perhaps some of the checklists may be reused by the reader.

Dr Gary Kroehnert

Public speakers need the ability to accept the things that they can't change,
the courage to change the things that they can change,
and the cunning to recognise the difference.

CHAPTER 1

The principles of adult learning and retention

The term 'learning' has many interpretations, but is generally accepted as a change in behaviour or attitude. It's not intended that in this chapter we analyse the theories behind adult learning, but it is intended to put forward some of the accepted principles of adult learning. The principles listed here are basically the same as those put forward in any 'methods instruction' or 'presentation skills' course; the only difference is that the principles will vary in name. If we want the information in our presentations to be retained we must understand these principles. However, if we are giving a presentation as entertainment, these points may not be as relevant.

These principles deal with training and education, and are common to the formal classroom setting as well as on-the-job training. Any form of training should include as many of these nine principles as possible.

We can easily remember the nine principles of learning by using the mnemonic RAMP 2 FAME.

R   Recency
A   Appropriateness
M   Motivation
P   Primacy

2   2-way communication

F   Feedback
A   Active learning
M   Multi-sense learning
E   Exercise

Nine principles

These principles are important in several ways. They allow you to prepare a presentation properly, to present efficiently and effectively, and to evaluate the presentation.

We will now look at the ideas behind these terms. It's important to note that these are not presented in a priority order—they all deserve equal consideration.

R: Recency

The law of Recency tells us that the things that are learned last are those best remembered by the participant. This applies in two separate areas of learning. Firstly, it applies to the content at the end of the presentation and, secondly, it applies to the things that are freshest in the participants' minds. For the first application, it's important for the presenter to summarise frequently and to ensure that the key messages are emphasised again at the end of the presentation. For the second application, it indicates that presenters should plan review sections into their presentations.

Factors to consider about Recency include:

- Keep each session of your presentation to a relatively short period of time, no longer than twenty minutes if possible.
- If presentations are longer than twenty minutes, recapitulate often. This breaks the larger presentation into smaller presentations with a lot of endings so that you can summarise.
- The end of every presentation is important. Recap the whole presentation, highlighting the key points or key messages.
- Keep the participants fully aware of the direction and progress of their learning.

A: Appropriateness

The law of Appropriateness says that all the information, training, training aids, case studies and other materials must be appropriate to the participants' needs. They can easily lose motivation if the presenter fails to keep the materials relevant to their needs. In addition, presenters must continually let participants know how the new information links with previous knowledge, so that we remove their fears of the unknown.

Factors to consider about Appropriateness include:

- The presenter should clearly identify a need for the participants to be taking part in the presentation. With this need identified the presenter must make sure that everything connected with the presentation is appropriate to that need.
- Use descriptions, examples or illustrations that the participants are familiar with.

M: Motivation

The law of Motivation shows us that the participants must want to learn, they must be ready to learn and there must be some reason to learn. Presenters find that if participants have strong motivation to learn, or a sense of purpose, they will excel in their learning. Once motivation has been created the learning atmosphere opens up. If we fail to use the law of Appropriateness and neglect to make the materials relevant, we will almost certainly lose participants' motivation.

Factors to consider about Motivation include:

- The material must be meaningful and worthwhile to the participant, and not only to the presenter.
- Not only must the participants be motivated, so must the presenter. If the presenter isn't motivated, learning probably won't take place.
- As mentioned in the law of Appropriateness, the presenter sometimes needs to identify a need for the participants to be there. Presenters can usually create motivation by telling the participants that this session can fill that need.
- Move from the known to the unknown. Start the session at a point the participants are familiar with. Gradually build up and link points together so that everyone knows where they are expected to go in the learning process.

P: Primacy

The law of Primacy states that the things participants learn first are usually learnt best, so the first impressions or pieces of information that participants get from the speaker are really important. For this reason it's good practice to include all of the key points at the beginning of the presentation. During the presentation expand on the key points and other associated information.

Also to be included with the law of Primacy is the fact that when participants are shown how to do something they must be shown the correct way the first time. The reason for this is that it's sometimes very difficult to 'unteach' participants if they get things wrong the first time.

Factors to consider about Primacy include:

- Again keep presentations to a relatively short period of time; twenty minutes is about right as suggested with the law of Recency.
- The beginning of your presentation will be important as you know most of the participants will be listening; so make it interesting and put a lot of important information into it.
- Keep the participants fully aware of the direction and progress of their learning.
- Ensure that participants get things right the first time you require them to do something.

2: 2-way communication

The law of 2-way communication quite clearly states that the information-delivery process involves communication *with* the participants, and not *at* them. Any form of presentation should be a 2-way communication. This doesn't necessarily mean that the whole session should be a discussion, but it must allow for interaction between the presenter/trainer/facilitator and the trainee/participant.

Factors to consider about 2-way communication include:

- Your body language is also included in 2-way communication: make sure it matches what you're saying.
- Your session plan should have interactions with the participants designed into it.

F: Feedback

The law of Feedback informs us that both the facilitator and the participant need information from each other. The facilitator needs to know that the participants are following and keeping pace and the participants need feedback on the standard of their performance.

Reinforcement is also required with feedback. If we reward participants (positive reinforcement) for doing things right, we have a far greater chance of getting them to change their behaviour to a desired outcome. Be aware, though, that too many negative reinforcements may not have the final response required.

Factors to consider about Feedback include:

- Trainees or participants should be tested frequently for presenter feedback.
- When participants are tested they must get feedback on their performance as soon as possible.
- Testing can also include the presenter asking frequent questions of the group.
- All feedback doesn't have to be positive, as some people believe. Positive feedback is only half of it, and is almost useless without negative feedback.
- When a participant does or says something right, acknowledge it (in front of the group if possible).
- Prepare your presentations so that there is positive reinforcement built into it at the very beginning.
- Look for someone doing it right as well as looking for someone doing it wrong.

A: Active learning

The law of Active Learning shows us that participants learn more when they are actively involved in the process. Remember the saying 'we learn by doing'?

This is important in the training of adults, particularly if we want them to retain information. If you want to instruct a group in writing reports, don't just tell them how it should be done—get them to do it. Another benefit of this is that adults are generally not used to sitting in a classroom setting all day, so the use of active learning will assist you in keeping them awake.

Factors to consider about Active Learning include:

- Use practical exercises during the instruction.
- Use plenty of questions during the instruction.
- A quick quiz may be used to keep the participants active.
- If at all possible get the participants to do what they are being instructed in.
- If the participants are kept sitting for long periods without any participation or questions being asked of them, it's possible for them to nod off or lose interest in the session.

M: Multiple-sense learning

The law of Multiple-sense Learning says that learning is far more effective if the participants use more than one of their five senses. If you tell participants about a new type of sandwich filling they may remember it. If you show them the product they probably will remember it. If you let them touch, smell and taste it as well, there is no way they will forget about it.

Avoid the dangers of boredom by keeping your group alert with multiple-sense learning

Factors to consider about Multiple-sense Learning include:

- If you tell participants about something, try to show them as well.
- Use as many of the participants' senses as necessary for them to learn, but don't get carried away.
- When using multiple-sense learning, make sure that the sense selected can be used. Ensure that it's not difficult for the group to hear, see and touch whatever it is you want them to.

I hear and I forget,
I see and I remember,
I do and I understand.
Confucius c. 450 BC

E: Exercise

The law of Exercise indicates that things that are repeated are best remembered. The law of Exercise is also referred to as overlearning or meaningful repetition. By getting participants to exercise or repeat new information we are increasing the possibility of them being able to recall that information at a later time. Multiplication tables learnt at school are one example of the law of Exercise. It's best if the presenter or facilitator can encourage exercise, or overlearning, by repeating information in different ways. Perhaps the presenter could talk about the new process or item, then show an overhead or diagram, show the finished product and finally get the participants to carry out the required task several times. Exercise also includes intensity.

Factors to consider about Exercise include:

- The more we get our participants to repeat something the more likely they are to retain the information.
- By asking frequent questions we are encouraging exercise or overlearning.
- The participants must perform the exercise themselves. Taking notes doesn't count in most cases, but it certainly won't do any harm.
- Summarise frequently as this is another form of exercise. Always summarise at the conclusion of a session.
- Get the participants to recall frequently what has been covered in the presentation.
- The law of Exercise also includes giving the participants exercises to carry out.

It's often stated that without some form of exercise, participants will forget one-quarter of what they have learnt within six hours, one-third within twenty-four hours and around ninety per cent within six weeks.

Conclusion

These principles of learning relate to training, education and facilitation. They are used in all areas whether in a classroom setting, on-the-job or in an auditorium. They can be used with children and adolescents as well as adults. Effective facilitation and instruction should use as many of these principles as possible, if not all of them. When you plan a presentation or session, look through the draft to make sure that these principles have been used and, if they haven't, maybe a revision is in order.

Recency	We have used recency a number of times during the session by breaking the larger session down into a number of smaller sessions.
Appropriateness	We have made the material appropriate to the participants at the beginning of the session.
Motivation	We have given the group reasons to be here and to listen to us, it has been made relevant to them.
Primacy	We have used the primacy effect a number of times during the session the same way we did with recency. We have broken the session up to give us lots of 'ends'. Note that the total session uses primacy and recency as well by using a properly structured beginning and conclusion.
2-way communication	We have allowed for, and encouraged, communication between the presenter and the participants. It has been designed into the session.
Feedback	We have allowed for feedback during the whole session. Positive reinforcement has also been designed into the beginning of the session to encourage participation.
Active learning	Both the presenter and the participants are constantly moving around and doing things.
Multi-sense learning	We have included multi-sense learning by using hearing, sight and touch.
Exercise	This has been exercised by getting the participants to not only listen, but also to watch, do and practise.

Application example

To give an effective presentation on applying arm slings (using the principles of learning), it was decided to use the following format:

- Motivational introduction, to include objectives and overview of the session.
- Link back to previous sessions.

- Tell participants how it is done.
- Show participants how it is done.
- Get participants to repeat (under control).
- Participants to practise on each other.
- Praise good work done by participants.
- Evaluation (testing of objectives).
- Summarise at end of session.
- Emphasise the key points.
- Link forward to next session.

Looking at the above we can see that the nine principles of adult learning have been used.

Further reading

Baird, L., Schneier, C. & Laird, D., *The Training and Development Sourcebook*, 2nd edn, Human Resource Press, Massachusetts, 1994.

Kroehnert, Gary, *Basic Training for Trainers*, 2nd edn, McGraw-Hill Book Co, Sydney, 1995.

Laird, Dugan, *Approaches to Training and Development*, 2nd edn, Addison-Wesley Publishing Company, Massachusetts, 1985.

Rogers, Jennifer, *Adults Learning*, 2nd edn, Open University Press, England, 1979, Chapters 1, 2 & 3.

CHAPTER 2

Location of presentations

The location, or venue, is of major importance to both the presenter and the attendees. Unfortunately, the venue is not always given the attention it deserves; it tends to be taken for granted. For information to be absorbed or for learning to take place effectively, we need to create a comfortable learning atmosphere.

Traditionally we think about classrooms or training rooms when we talk about presentations, education or learning. But what about the possibility of conducting outdoor-based programs or activities? For information to be absorbed or for learning to take place effectively, we need to create not only a comfortable learning environment, but an appropriate one.

On page 10 is a comprehensive checklist for indoor venues. It may include items that the experienced presenter may not be concerned with but the new presenter will find it worthwhile checking all of the items listed.

Probably one of the most important features that presenters would like to see incorporated in room design is the flexibility to arrange the room as a lecture theatre, or a discussion room, or as a number of workstation areas. Unfortunately, we are not given this opportunity very often as we would tend to exceed everyone's budget.

If given the opportunity to choose or modify a venue, there are a number of things the presenter must take into consideration. Listed below are the items that we need to think of.

The number of participants generally determines the location. A decision about the location should be the presenter's first priority. Don't try to squeeze a few more into an already crowded venue; cut the number down or get another location. A crowded venue will not set the proper learning atmosphere. Similarly, a large room with only a few people can also create a barrier to learning.

The size of the room will generally depend on two factors: what the room is being used for and the number of people it has to accommodate. If the room is being used in a classroom setting (a chair with arm tables), allow about 1.5 to 2.5 square metres per person. If the room is being used in a

```
┌─────────────────────────────────────────────────────────────┐
│                                                               │
│   VENUE CHECKLIST                                             │
│  ───────────────────────────────────────────────────────     │
│   Number of participants                            _____  │
│   Size of room                                      _____  │
│   Arrangement of room                               _____  │
│   Suitable chairs and tables                        _____  │
│   Arrangement of furniture                          _____  │
│   Lighting                                          _____  │
│   Noise                                             _____  │
│   Temperature                                       _____  │
│   Access                                            _____  │
│   Facilities                                        _____  │
│   Distractions on walls                             _____  │
│   Distractions outside                              _____  │
│   Acoustic qualities                                _____  │
│   Power outlets                                     _____  │
│   Extension leads                                   _____  │
│   Overhead projector                                _____  │
│   Whiteboard and markers                            _____  │
│   Video and monitor                                 _____  │
│   Projection equipment                              _____  │
│   Spares                                            _____  │
│   Public address system                             _____  │
│   Storage area                                      _____  │
│                                                               │
│   _____                  _____  │
│   _____                  _____  │
│   _____                  _____  │
│   _____                  _____  │
│                                                               │
└─────────────────────────────────────────────────────────────┘
```

conference setting (chairs and full tables) allow about 2.0 to 2.5 square metres per person. A simple method of estimating the size of the room needed is to multiply the number of participants by the area required per person, then add a bit for yourself and your equipment. It is possible to find many other specifications for conference room sizes, but they vary greatly. An alternative is to use a room that is a size you and the group feel comfortable with. For your first few presentations check with an experienced presenter in your organisation, or someone you know, for advice on room sizes and limits to participants in your conference rooms. The information given to you will probably be close to the first alternative described.

The arrangement of the room generally needs to suit the presentation or the program. Try to keep things looking tidy. If you're conducting a lecture keep the front of the room clear for the lecturer. If there will be a lot of small-group work, arrange the seating roughly where you want the groups to be located. Ensure that the arrangements allow for everyone to see and hear adequately.

Suitable chairs and tables are needed for a classroom situation. The chairs must be comfortable but firm. (If they are too comfortable, you may lose a few participants as they nod off.) The tables should be narrow and long, about 0.5 by 1.5 metres, which allows the participants to sit two wide along the table on one side. Don't be tempted to increase the number of participants by sitting them on both sides of the table, as it gets too crowded.

The arrangement of chairs and tables generally sets the scene for the participants. If they see the chairs set in a circle they should expect a lot of group discussion. If they see the chairs set in rows they could expect that the person giving the presentation will be doing most of the work.

The lighting in the room must be arranged to provide for both the presenter's and audience requirements. The presenter needs light for the whiteboard to be seen (but not so much that it becomes hard for the attendees to see the overhead projector screen). The audience also needs enough light to be able to take notes if they require. It is up to the individual presenter to determine the appropriate lighting requirements.

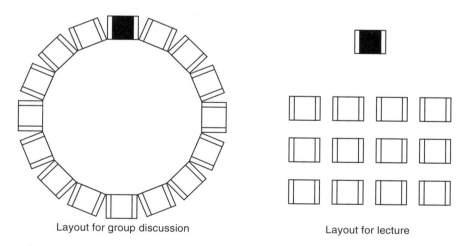

Layout for group discussion   Layout for lecture

Seating arrangements should be suitable for the intended presentation method

Noise in the background during any type of presentation can be very destructive to the learning atmosphere. Most presenters would like to have a totally soundproof room without any windows, but unfortunately this type of room is rare. What we can do, though, is locate the room far enough away from the work area to exclude work noises such as machines and telephones.

The temperature of the room must be comfortable for the majority of the group. Don't try to satisfy everyone, you won't be able to. Keep the temperature between 20°C and 25°C if possible, and also allow for gentle air circulation in the room. Another thing to remember is that some presentation aids generate heat during their use, and your cooling equipment must be able to handle this problem. It is strongly recommended that smoking be banned in any presentation situation. Not only might the smoke be hard on your voice but some of the other participants might feel very uncomfortable with it. Obviously with some presentations, such as weddings, engagements, birthday parties and so on, it may not be appropriate to ask people to put out their cigarettes. Commonsense would prevail in these situations.

Access is something that most people now take for granted, but we do need to consider how the audience will get to the venue. Will public transport be sufficient? If they use their own transport will they have somewhere to park? We must also consider access for people with disabilities, such as ramps for wheelchairs.

The facilities that we usually now take for granted must be checked by the presenter. Are tea and coffee making facilities available for morning and afternoon breaks? Do we have access to telephones? Do we know where all the toilets are located? Do we know where the fire exits are? All of this information might need to be passed on to the participants at the beginning of the presentation. It may also be necessary to find out if there is residential accommodation available.

Distractions, apart from noise and temperature, might also be present. Participants can find irrelevant posters and paintings on the walls a distraction. A room painted an unusual colour can be a distraction. Windows can be a source of participant distraction, so check to see if blinds can be used to reduce this. A crowded room can be a distraction and the presenter must fix this before training starts. Anything that is not required for the presentation should be removed from the venue so as not to attract attention.

The acoustic qualities of the location should assist the leader in keeping control of the group. The presenter's voice should be the dominant noise in the room. If the acoustics are good, background noise should be minimal. The noise from background conversation and projectors should be absorbed by the room, and not be in competition with the speaker.

Power outlets must be checked for availability and location. If you are going to present in a new location, check the power outlets. Their location may affect your arrangement of the room.

Presentation aids must be checked to see that the ones you want to use are available. Some conference facilities have only a limited type and quantity. When you establish that the presentation aids you require are available, check to make sure they are in top working condition. And do it yourself—don't take anyone else's word for it.

Spares must be located and you will need to know how to fit them. Overhead projectors, film projectors and slide projectors, for example, might have a globe burn out while you are using them. Prompt replacement means the least disruption.

A public address system may be advisable in a large conference or seminar situation. It could be a portable type or a built-in system. If you believe that all of the people in the group will not be able to hear the speakers properly, you must make enquiries into the use of the public address system.

Storage areas could be needed for excess equipment, handout materials, presentation aids not in use, spare parts, models and many other items.

| Conclusion

The venue needs to have a learning or listening atmosphere created by the speaker. If you don't create this atmosphere, there may be a barrier which prevents learning from taking place or information from being retained.

The venue doesn't need to have state-of-the-art equipment, but it does need to be a suitable size for the group and be set out to suit the use intended. The design should be flexible to some extent, allow for adequate ventilation, have satisfactory lighting and have suitable facilities. This would be the minimum standard that public speakers should allow for the participants as well as for themselves.

With some venues, presenters need to use their imagination and creativity to overcome some enormous problems so that they can create a suitable learning climate. Without this atmosphere you may as well pack up and go home.

Application example

Next month you are required to conduct a presentation for your organisation in an unfamiliar city. To find a suitable venue you will first need to determine the number of participants who will be attending. This will allow you to work out roughly what size room is needed.

With this information it is now possible to contact a number of locations and request full information about their facilities. When you receive the information you will be able to go through your checklist and check off most of the items. This will generally be enough information to make a decision on which venue to use.

It is your responsibility to check the outstanding items at the location before any presentation commences.

Further reading

Baird, L., Schneier, C. & Laird, D., *The Training and Development Sourcebook*, 2nd edn, Human Resource Press, Massachusetts, 1994.

Craig, Robert, *Training and Development Handbook*, 4th edn, McGraw-Hill Book Company, New York, 1996.

Laird, Dugan, *Approaches to Training and Development*, 2nd edn, Addison-Wesley Publishing Company, Massachusetts, 1985.

CHAPTER 3

Researching a topic

In this chapter we will be looking at the research that may be required in preparation for the presentation of a new topic.

Research into a topic is generally conducted for at least two reasons. Firstly, to supply information for the session to be presented and, secondly, to give the researcher some expert information on the topic.

Why is research necessary?

The participants must be given correct and up-to-date information in each presentation they attend. The best way for the speaker to find out if it is correct and up to date is to spend some time researching the relevant facts.

Careful research makes for a well-prepared presenter

Also, the participants rightly expect the speaker to know the topics being presented thoroughly. Would you sit and listen attentively to a person who did not appear to know the subject? This means that the presenter must carry out study before entering the room. Experienced presenters will tell you that unless the subject matter is completely understood by them they cannot effectively plan their presentation or communicate confidently to the participants.

Don't think that you have to be a walking encyclopaedia, or an authority on every subject you will be presenting. But you must know more subject information than is to be presented to the participants. You will find that this information is needed to answer some of the questions that will be asked. Considering the rate at which information is currently being generated on most topics, we probably all find that we simply haven't got the time to keep totally up to date.

If you find that you are asked a question relevant to the topic and you don't know the answer to it, tell the group that you don't know but that you will find out and report back to them later.

What methods are available?

Sources of research for a presentation may include:

- activity figures, such as production, sales, wastage, quality control
- staff performance appraisal records
- job analysis, including job descriptions and work study reports
- relevant policies and procedures
- interview records with the employees, their supervisors and any other personnel involved
- personnel evaluations, such as employee test results, questionnaires, lists of identified competencies
- the workplace itself, such as equipment, supplies, technology, work processes, raw material, etc.
- corporate plans, such as for new technology, expansion or contraction, diversification, mergers
- accident reports and statistics.

While these sources provide ample information for a training needs analysis they may provide only a small amount of information on a particular topic or subject. Perhaps this information is ample for your needs, but if you find that you require more information on your subject, a few more research sources are listed here for you.

A library can provide bulk information, but trying to wade through it all can be a problem in itself. Don't try to read and understand it all; ask the librarian for assistance in narrowing your broad topic down to a manageable size. Computers may also be used effectively for this purpose. Not all libraries

Presenters must learn how to confine their research to a useable quantity

carry the same books; most specialise in different subjects. Make sure you find out which one you need to visit.

A film library may give you a change of pace for your research and presentation. If you find a relevant film or video on your topic you may decide to use it in your presentation after you have previewed it. The number of film libraries is continually increasing and they are relatively easy to locate.

Advertisements in the magazines and publications you subscribe to may give you other starting points for sources of information.

The human resources section may be able to tell you of employees who are knowledgeable in the subject you are researching. If the information required is job related, they may even be able to give you the names of retired personnel who worked in certain areas for a number of years. These people can be a tremendous source of information.

Specialists who are known to have information in your subject may be contacted. Consultants and professional educators are examples of such specialists but the main problem is trying to get them to give you some of their time. You may find that some specialists have their own libraries of books and films. As these have already been selectively chosen they could also be of use, particularly if you can get recommendations from the specialist as to which ones you need to look at.

Old records located in your organisation can unveil relevant reference documents and, if you're lucky, perhaps some slides or photographs you may be able to use in your presentation.

Relevant trades areas normally have condensed information in booklet form that may be used for your research. You may also find that they have produced films or videos that could be of value to you and your participants.

Government agencies that deal with training, education and employment are also useful sources of information. It may take some time to find what you're looking for, but it will generally be worth the effort.

Staff are often overlooked as sources of information for your research. Have you ever asked the people around you what qualifications and experience they have? Ask them sometime—you may get a pleasant surprise.

Family and friends should be checked with as well. They could have more information for you, particularly for the social type of presentations.

If you have used more than a couple of these sources for your research, you may find that you now have so much information you don't know how you're going to present it all. The solution is easy—you don't present it all. What you need to do now is to sort all of your expert research information into different categories. You want to select the information the audience *must* know to be able to carry out what will be required of them. This 'must know' type of information wouldn't necessarily apply to social presentations, such as a farewell speech, but would certainly apply to information-type presentations to people in the workplace. On second thought, maybe it is appropriate for the farewell speech!

You may find that before you start your research it is worthwhile designing some type of filing system. As you find sources of information for particular topics (not necessarily the one you are currently researching), record them on a topic card or something similar. You may find at a later date that you need to research a topic that is already in your files. If so, some of the hard work is already done for you.

Conclusion

It is important for you as the presenter to know as much about the subject matter as would be expected by the participants. If you want to have any credibility with them, and if you want them to become involved and motivated, you need to become more than just conversant with the subject material.

The research exercise can become very tiring in some cases. However, if you're asked, or told, to present a session where you don't know the topic material very well, it's definitely in your best interests to research the material thoroughly.

You may find that when you start your research, the job is easiest if you break your large topic area into smaller specific subtopics. This will save a lot of time as you will only be dealing with relevant information.

When you finish your research remember to cull the information you have collected so that you finish up with only the material that the participants must know in connection with the topic. If you have more presentation time than is required, you may start giving them some of the secondary information, but remember that it's better to teach or give a small amount well than to teach or give a large amount not so well.

Application example

Let's say that you have been given the job of researching a presentation on 'Safe lifting practices in the workplace'. Assuming that you had very little knowledge of the topic, what sources would you use to carry out your research?

If you go back over the sources listed in this chapter, you should be able to identify at least fifteen separate sources. In addition to those listed you could probably think of at least half a dozen more. See how easy it is to become overloaded with research information?

Now comes the step of refining the information down to that which is essential to the participants. With the information sorted, you may now prepare your presentation being confident that you have a more than satisfactory knowledge of the material.

Further reading

Craig, Robert, *Training and Development Handbook*, 4th edn, McGraw-Hill Book Company, New York, 1996, Chapter 44.

Kalish, Karen, *How To Give A Terrific Presentation*, Amacom, New York, 1997.

CHAPTER 4

Objectives

This chapter is probably one of the most important in this book, particularly for someone giving an information-type presentation or for the new trainer. The reason for making such a strong statement is that, without clearly stated objectives, the presenter or the trainer and the audience may have absolutely no idea of where they are heading. If they don't know where they are heading, how can they know when they have reached their target? Very simply, an objective, or a number of objectives, give us our target, or learning goals. This target or goal will apply to the individual presentation or session or to the course of instruction as a whole. In a training course, all of the presentation or session objectives taken together should equal the course objective/s.

All objectives are normally designed and written after the needs analysis has been completed, and the decision to go ahead with the program has been made. The needs analysis is the process someone goes through to indicate that a presentation or training course is required.

We will be talking in later chapters about using 'road maps' for the design and delivery of your presentations. If we apply the idea of a road map to this chapter our objective is the finishing point.

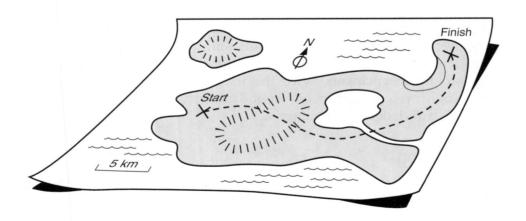

Make sure that you map out the course you intend a presentation to take

Keep the aims and objectives of the session clearly in mind

The difference between aims and objectives

Even experienced presenters and trainers can become confused between aims and objectives. Aims and objectives are not the same thing. An aim normally consists of a statement of general intent. It may use an item or example to represent the final approvable behaviour of the participant at the conclusion of the course or workshop. By contrast, an objective states the requirements in precise terms. An example of this might be:

Session aim: To develop an awareness and understanding of the different types of training methods.

Session objective: By the end of this session participants will be able to list correctly at least twenty different training methods (stating one advantage and disadvantage for each) using the notes provided.

The above example shows that the aim simply states a general intent which would probably be useful in promoting or selling the course or workshop to the management or the participants. An aim is generally all that is required for an impromptu speech or for a social-type presentation. The session objective would normally be given to the participants at the beginning of the session so that they know exactly what is required of them by the end of the session.

To use the road map analogy again: the aim tells us what town we are going to; the objective tells us which street, what time we need to be there and what the road conditions are.

When do we need objectives?

Objectives are only usually required for formal training presentations or sessions.

After it has been established that someone needs training, we know in a general way, what subjects or topics need to be included in the training program from the results of the needs analysis. When we know what subject matter is to be covered, we need to sit down and write general instructional objectives for the course, followed by specific session objectives for each separate session.

We can't start to write any of the teaching material for the course until we have established the session objectives, otherwise we risk the chance of the information being on the wrong track. How do we know which road to take if we don't know where we're going? As well as being important for the trainer, when specific objectives are stated to the group members, they can also be certain in which direction we should all be headed. How many times have you been sitting in a presentation and had absolutely no idea where the presenter was heading, or when or if they had reached the objective of the session?

If we use other presenters in the session, they will know what the outcome must be if we give them specific session objectives. Without these objectives they won't know what exactly needs to be covered.

An example of this may be the situation where we ask a fellow trainer to present a session on 'video recorders' and he or she delivers a session on 'how a video recorder operates'. What was really wanted should have been described in a clearly stated objective. 'At the end of this session the participants must be able to label the components in a given diagram of a video recorder with 100 per cent accuracy.' See how much easier the task has been made for everyone?

Another important issue for using course and session objectives is that it gives us a base for any form of evaluation or test we intend applying. If we state our objective clearly it tells us what the evaluation must be. If the test or evaluation doesn't tie in exactly with the objectives, one of them must be modified so that they do match each other.

How do we write an objective?

Probably the hardest thing about training is to formulate the session or the course objectives. We must assume that if we put all of the session objectives together, they will equal the course objective.

All objectives should be stated in terms of observable behaviour or performance and should not merely describe what the participants have learnt or become familiar with during the time allocated for the course.

Secondly, an objective should be measurable in some form so that we can set our tests from it. It can therefore be said that objectives should be both observable and measurable.

It is generally believed that reaching our session objectives will eventually lead to us achieving the desired behavioural change or attitude change.

Writing objectives can be confusing at first for the new presenter and not all experienced trainers and presenters find writing objectives a simple task. It may be simplest to start writing your objectives by filling in the missing spaces in the formula below:

By the end of this session the trainee will be able to:

_____ (an action word) _____

_____ (item) _____

_____ (condition) _____

_____ (standard) _____

The *action word* is something we can observe; the *item* is normally an object or item from our session; the *condition* is what is given and describes any variables; and the *standard* is our measurable criteria. (To help you there is a list of terms you can select from at the end of this chapter.) To give you an example:

By the end of this session the trainee will be able to:

underline (an action word)

the nouns (item)

given a printed list of statements (condition)

and have at least 80 per cent correct. (standard)

Another one:

By the end of this session the trainee will be able to:

total (an action word)

a list of numbers (item)

given a prepared sheet and a calculator (condition)

and have at least 90 per cent correct. (standard)

One more:

By the end of this session the trainee will be able to:

assemble (an action word)

the parts of an overhead projector (item)

given all of the parts in a box and without the aid of a manufacturer's manual. (condition)

The project must be in assembled working order within ten minutes. (standard)

Just to make sure:

> By the end of this session the trainee will be able to:
>
> demonstrate (an action word)
>
> the procedure for assembling a DT5 (item)
>
> given all of the unassembled parts and the manufacturer's technical manuals (condition)
>
> to the manufacturer's specification within three hours. (standard)

And finally:

> By the end of this session the trainee will be able to:
>
> count (an action word)
>
> the number of needles in a haystack (item)
>
> given a haystack, a magnet, a magnifying glass and a box of bandaids. (condition)
>
> The counting must be completed within twelve hours and must be correct. (standard)

Conclusion

A general aim is all that is required for most social presentations. Objectives, however, are required for all formal training sessions. Why should we use objectives in training?

- They provide direction.
- They provide guidelines for testing.
- They convey instructional intent to others.

When we sit down to write our objectives we must ensure that we set realistic goals. The objectives must be achievable within the constraints placed on us, whether these relate to time, resources, facilities or any other factor likely to affect the final outcome.

After the results of the needs analysis have been interpreted, we can state that certain objectives have to be reached within the program. Nearly all objectives are set after we have conducted the needs analysis.

We also use our stated objectives to set the test criteria, which must match them. It's not uncommon for the test to be written straight after the objectives have been designed. With these start and finish points established, it becomes relatively easy to fill in the gap. With this method we can be certain that the test is in line with the objective.

A well-written and easily understood objective must:

- state something about the end of the session or the end of training
- say something about the trainee, not the instructor or the course
- include an input or a condition

List of common action words

add	arrange	assemble	bend
build	calculate	carry	catch
choose	circle	collect	colour
compute	construct	count	cut
demonstrate	describe	design	divide
draw	fold	identify	illustrate
indicate	label	lift	list
mark	match	modify	multiply
name	perform	pick	place
plan	point	punctuate	rearrange
recall	recite	rewrite	ride
run	select	separate	smile
solve	spell	state	swim
tabulate	taste	throw	translate
underline	use	walk	write

List of common terms for standards

Accurate to _____ decimal points
At least 8 out of 10 attempts
At least _____ per cent correct
At least _____ within an hour
At _____ per hour
Before sunset
Having all correct
In the specified sequence
Not acceptable if safety procedures are violated
With at least _____ correct
Within _____ minutes
Within _____ tolerance
Without error
With no more than _____ errors

List of common terms for equipment to use (conditions)

Given a checklist, notes and manual
Given a complete technical manual
Given a set of blueprints
Given a slide rule
Standing on your head
Under simulated conditions
Using all of the parts
Using any equipment needed
Using the machine practised on
Using your notes
Without the use of a manual
Without the use of a calculator
With the aid of a checklist

- have single outcomes
- state a performance by using action words
- include a standard to be achieved by the trainee
- be stated in such a way that there is no doubt as to what is required.

At the conclusion of a course or session that may be conducted again, it is good practice for the presenter to consider revising the objective. It may be that the objective, as stated, is unachievable or is not challenging enough. Review it while the experience of the training is still fresh in your mind.

The final list of objectives should contain outcomes that are considered essential for the participants to achieve. These objectives are usually the minimum standards for the participant to reach. It may be that they are the minimum requirements needed for the participant to move on to the next area of learning.

I deliberately have not used any quotations so far in this book. Sometimes they seem inappropriate and serve merely to fill up space. However, I have a quote for you now as I believe that this is a very relevant statement made by an expert on objectives, Robert Mager, in his book *Preparing Instructional Objectives*.

> *The purpose of the objective is to communicate something to somebody.*
> *If that somebody doesn't get the message as intended, don't argue or defend—fix it!*

Don't get hung up on the terms unless it's required specifically for some reason. The main thing is to make sure it's all covered!

Application example

Some years ago a trainer I know was asked to develop a train-the-trainer course. After a needs analysis had been carried out, it appeared that there were several topic areas requiring certain amounts of information. When all this information had been gathered and sorted, session objectives had to be written and were given to the presenting trainers. The trainers, having been given these specific session objectives, then knew the goal/s they, and the trainees, had to reach by the end of the sessions. The following are a few of the session objectives that were written and handed over to the trainers.

- By the end of this session the participants will be able to state (without referring to notes) at least fifteen items that need to be taken into consideration for a training venue.
- By the end of this session the participants will be able to demonstrate

correctly (without reference) the assembly and operation of a video camera and recorder in the training room.

- By the end of this session the participants will be able to write a set of session notes for a given topic using the sample format that will be handed out. The finished notes must be understood by the instructor without explanation.

Are all of these objectives stated correctly?

Further reading

Baird, L., Schneier, C. & Laird, D., *The Training and Development Sourcebook*, 2nd edn, Human Resource Press, Massachusetts, 1994.

Donaldson, Les & Scannell, Edward, Human *Resource Development: The New Trainer's Guide*, 2nd edn, Addison-Wesley Publishing Company, Massachusetts, 1986, Chapter 4.

Gronlund, Norman, *How to Write Instructional Objectives*, 4th edn, Macmillan Publishing, New York, 1990.

Hughes, Shirley, *Professional Presentations*, McGraw-Hill Book Company, Sydney, 1990.

Laird, Dugan, *Approaches to Training and Development*, 2nd edn, Addison-Wesley Publishing Company, Massachusetts, 1985.

Mager, Robert, *Preparing Instructional Objectives*, 2nd edn, Pitman Learning Company, California, 1984.

CHAPTER 5

Presenting a skill

The formal lecture or presentation has little use in skill or practical training, as muscular and manual activities demand that learning is done by doing.

In a skill training session the presenter must aim to have the participants perform the skill correctly the first time. Another aim should be to get the participants to develop smooth, confident and easy movements when performing the skill. During the skill session the presenter must also promote accuracy, speed and quality.

This chapter will look at two topics dealing with the presentation of a skill. They are:

- What is a skill?
- How do you go about presenting a skill correctly?

A practical demonstration is essential when you are teaching a skill

On pages 37–8 is a copy of a skill session sheet which may be of use to the skills presenter or trainer.

What is a skill?

A skill is a complex sequence of practical activities. Some examples of skills include typing, washing up, cleaning a whiteboard, plugging in an overhead projector or turning on a light.

Some skills are far more complex than others. Some may only involve simple motions, such as turning on an overhead projector. Others may involve use of the senses, such as determining whether an overhead image is being projected squarely onto the screen or not. The more complex type of skill could involve understanding and knowledge, for example, the ability to read the operating instructions of the overhead projector and understand them.

It can be seen that almost everything that is done using some form of motion is a skill. As most activities use all three types of skills—motor, perceptual and cognitive—we will deal with them as a combined activity. This combination of motor, perceptual and cognitive skills is given the term 'psychomotor skill'. Regardless of the type of skill that you may be instructing, the rules remain the same.

Skills training always involves the same basic rules

| Presenting a skill correctly

The complete presentation process involves four sections:
- preparation
- presentation
- student practice
- assessment.

We will look at all of these sections in one process as they must go hand-in-hand.

The steps:

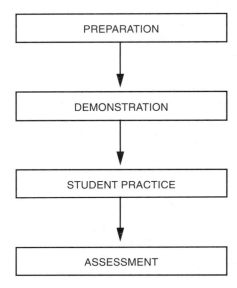

The presenter's procedure should follow the demonstration—practice sequence for any skills training

The preparation

There is a great deal the presenter must do before presenting a skill to any group. Some of the items that need to be attended to will include the following:
- establishing the current level of knowledge of the audience in the given topic/subject as they may not have the prerequisite knowledge to perform the skill
- discussing the skill with other 'experts', analysing the skill and breaking it down

- drafting a plan to be followed for the presentation so all relevant points can be covered in logical sequence
- preparing all presentation support materials such as overhead transparencies, handouts, samples, films, videos, models, project lists, examinations, marking guides, etc.
- preparing lesson objectives and building in links back and forward to other areas of instruction or other fields
- preparation of an introduction—a good introduction will gain attention, arouse interest in the demonstration, and check existing knowledge.

The presenter's personal preparation is a major part of skill training

This is not intended to be a comprehensive list of items to be carried out by the presenter, but it does show that the presenter has to be prepared in many ways to demonstrate a skill correctly and professionally.

Practical instruction is like an iceberg, in that the part that is visible (conducting a demonstration and supervising student practice) makes only a small part of the effort. The bulk of the work goes on beforehand. (Field 1984)

The presentation

The presentation must be done correctly. How can anyone expect your audience to do it correctly if you can't?

There are a few methods suggested for the sequence of presentations. We will be discussing the one that tends to be the most commonly referred to in current texts, and is being used by many adult colleges.

The method has seven basic steps. They are easy to follow and they also cover the final two sections of our process, student practice and assessment.

1. **Present at normal speed**

   Present the skill correctly, at normal speed, so that your audience can see the final result and can also see what is expected from them at the conclusion of the presentation.

2. **Present again slowly**

   Present again for the audience, this time doing it slowly so that they can see exactly what is being done. As the presenter demonstrates, the individuals in the audience should begin to recognise names, parts, tools and any obvious skills.

   When demonstrating and explaining how the skill is performed, presenters must be careful about what they say and how they say it. The presenter should introduce each step, then highlight the key points with deliberate and possibly exaggerated movements. These key points can also be highlighted by voice, by giving reasons, or perhaps by repetition. It's a good idea to pause between key points to let them sink in. The presenter must have a set of notes or a 'skill sheet' to follow for this part of the demonstration. The skill sheet gives a complete breakdown of the skill with the key points highlighted and any 'tricks of the trade' and safety points noted.

3. **Verbal instruction from the group**

   Now get the group to tell you how to carry out the task in the correct sequence. The presenter carries out the performance as instructed by the audience.

Student practice

4. **Controlled audience performance**

   Have the group carry out the skill under close supervision and at a controlled pace. It is important that the individuals perform this exercise correctly. It is difficult, and sometimes almost impossible, to counteract the effects of a skill learned incorrectly.

5. **Student practice**

   Now is the time for group practice. This part of a skill session should be at least 50 per cent of the allocated session time. During this time the presenter must be available to answer any questions that arise. If an individual in your group has problems, don't take over from them but get them to fix it themselves; the presenter or other members of the group can give the correct information or suggestions. Try to enlist their peers to assist with any problems.

The assessment

6. Student assessment

Some form of assessment must take place to ensure that the individuals in the group have reached the stated objectives and standards that were described at the beginning of the session.

Assessment may be done during the session by asking questions, or it may be done at the end of the session by using some form of test (written, practical or other). The type of assessment generally depends on the presenter and the type of skill being instructed. The test could be, for example, getting the individuals to replace the globe in an overhead projector to the manufacturer's standards within fifteen seconds.

An important point with assessment is that the person being tested should be expecting the type of test you give. The test must also be relevant to the topic. If you are demonstrating how to change a globe in an overhead projector, then get them to change the globe. Don't give them a test that asks them to identify all of the parts of the projector.

7. Conclusion

The presentation must conclude with the demonstrator recapitulating the main points of the session, and clarifying any outstanding areas of concern. If possible, all test results should be made available before the end of the session, so they might be included in the conclusion.

Method for presenting a skill correctly
1. Present at normal speed
2. Present again slowly
3. Verbal instruction from the participants
4. Controlled participant performance
5. Student practice
6. Student assessment
7. Conclusion

Conclusion

The skill sheet has proven itself to be invaluable in the process of skills-based training. It ensures that the presenter covers all the relevant points in the correct sequence and it gives the key points and safety points at the right time. Presenters need to start out with clear objectives and must always be thinking of ways to motivate the participants to learn.

Presenters should design a skill sheet to suit their own needs. This is not uncommon and so there is a wide variety of types. Most of them are different and include only the information particular trainers or presenters require for their personal use.

Another important point to remember is that at least half the session time should be made available for the audience to perform and practise the skill. Also, remember that the first time the individuals in the group perform the skill it must be done correctly.

It is strongly suggested that the presenter practise the demonstration before giving the performance. It doesn't matter how well you think you know how to do it, sometimes the parts don't fit the way they should—so practise.

Application example

To trial this concept we gave a new instructor the task of demonstrating 'how to assemble and disassemble a scuba (Self Contained Underwater Breathing Apparatus) unit'. These particular skill sheets needed to be slightly different from most others as they were to be used by a number of scuba diving instructors and therefore had to be understood by all.

The first step for the instructor was to research the current information available on the particular subject, the main references being two instructor-level texts. These texts supplied only very basic information, which surprised

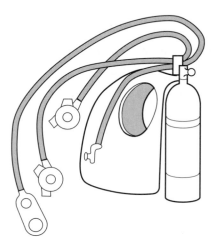

Skill training is applicable in a wide variety of situations

the presenters who had assumed that the information would be more comprehensive. On completion of that assignment the instructor spoke to two other experienced scuba diving instructors to obtain any relevant information they might have. This information was to highlight the safety points and tricks of the trade.

When the research and discussions had been finalised, it was time to practise performing the skill. While doing so the instructor made notes on the correct sequence to be followed by the students. These notes included a clearly stated objective, an opening introduction and a motivator for the group. As this set of notes was completed, a draft skill sheet was written to include the operations, key points and safety points. On completion of the main skill sheet, the front cover sheet was finalised and it included all the other necessary information, such as objectives, equipment needed, references and problems.

	Sheet no._____
Title/skill:	Assembly and disassembly of scuba equipment.
Objective/s:	By the end of this session students will be able to: 1. attach a BCD to the scuba tank so that the pack if snug, oriented in the proper direction, and placed at the correct height 2. attach a scuba regulator to a scuba tank so that the regulator hose is oriented to come over the right shoulder and the low pressure inflator is on the left 3. attach the low pressure inflator hose correctly onto the BCD and check the operation 4. demonstrate correct procedure for checking tank pressure and regulator operation 5. explain suggested actions for a high pressure O-ring leak and for a free-flowing regulator 6. correctly remove a regulator from a scuba tank and replace the dust cap on the regulator 7. correctly remove the BCD from the scuba tank and place both items on ground.
Equipment:	• 1 tank, regulator and BCD for each student and instructor. • spare O-rings.
Reference:	NAUI Professional Resource Organiser (1984) Openwater 1 scuba diver instructor guide
Problems:	Ensure regulators have low pressure inflator hoses. Ensure all tanks are fully charged.
Introduction:	If you want to be able to breathe underwater you must be able to assemble your equipment correctly. This equipment involves the use of high pressure air and if not used correctly can cause serious injury.

Scuba skill session sheet

	Sheet no. _____	
Operations	Key points	Safety
ASSEMBLE Position tank	• Stand tank up • O-ring facing away	• Don't leave tank standing unattended
Position BCD	• Slide over tank • BCD facing away • Height of BCD should be halfway up tank valve • Adjust to fit different size tanks (63 & 88) • Lock in position	• Avoid hitting head on tank valve • Must be secure so it doesn't fall out when straps are set
Position & attach regulator	• Remove dust cap • Regulator and octopus to right side • Machined face to O-ring • Do up finger tight • Connect low pressure inflator to BCD	• Keep out of sand • Check O-ring is there • If too tight cannot undo later • Pull knurled nut back

Turn air on	• Turn tank on
	
	• Check tank pressure
	• Check second stage regulator
	• Check octopus
	• Check LP inflator
		• Slowly check position of gauges
		  On and back half turn
		  What to do if O-ring missing
		• Must be full to commence dive
		• Must breathe easily
		
		• Must inflate and deflate

Lay down	• Gauges and regulators in front	• Keep out of sand and grass
DISMANTLE To turn off	• Turn air off • Purge lines	• Not over tight
Remove regulator	• Disconnect LP inflator • Undo nut • Replace dust cap • Place regulator away	• Must be dry
	Remove BCD • Undo velcro • Slide off tank • Place BCD away	• Hold tank
Tank	• Lay tank down	• So it won't fall
FINAL Rinse all equipment		• Don't push purge button

Scuba skill session sheet

The final skill sheet was included with the session notes, the presentation went ahead and the notes used by the new instructor worked well. To check that the notes were easily understood by other instructors it was decided to run the presentation a second time, with another instructor using the skill sheets. This again proved to be satisfactory, both for the instructor and the trainee.

	Sheet no. _____
Title/skill:	
Objective/s:	
Equipment:	
Reference:	
Problems:	
Introduction:	

Skill session sheet

Sheet no. _____

Operations	Key points	Safety

Skill session sheet

Further reading

Field, Laurie, *Skilling Australia*, Longman Cheshire, Melbourne, 1990.

Kroehnert, Gary, *Basic Training for Trainers*, 2nd Edn, McGraw-Hill Book Company, Sydney, 1995.

Pennington, F. C., *Assessing Educational Needs of Adults*, New Directions for Continuing Education Quarterly Sourcebooks, Jossey-Bass, San Francisco, 1980, Series No. 7.

Video: *You'll Soon Get The Hang Of It*, Video Arts.

Video: *Right First Time*, NSW TAFE.

CHAPTER 6

Presentation notes or session plans

In this chapter we will describe what presentation notes, session plans or lesson plans are, look at the reasons for having them and describe what they should include. At the end of this chapter you will find a sample presentation plan. It may be used until you choose to devise your own.

What are presentation notes or session plans?

Firstly, it must be stated that presentation notes, session plans, session notes, lesson plans and lesson notes are all the same thing. They are simply the road map we need to follow for the presentation. They ensure that the presenter or instructor heads towards the aim or objective/s of the presentation or lesson. They also enable the presenter or trainer to check in advance that the sequencing of the presentation is correct, the content relevant, and the presentation methods suitable. The presentation plan is also a checklist of the resources required for the presentation. Presentation plans are useful tools for speakers or instructors in any field.

A presentation plan is a set of notes in logical order for the presenter to follow to ensure that the objectives set for the presentation are met. A presentation plan also includes other relevant information, such as the presentation aids required, references and identified problem areas. A separate presentation plan should be used for each presentation because each has its own objectives and therefore requires separate planning. Generally, it is a requirement that the lesson objectives be reached by the participants before moving on to the next lesson for formal-type training presentations.

Why use presentation plans?

Why use a road map when going on a driving holiday? We would be able to start our journey without the road map, but we would not know where we were going, or if and when we had reached our destination. A presentation plan is very similar to a road map in that it shows us a starting point, a finishing point, and all the places we need to pass or explore along the way.

As well as giving the speaker or presenter a logical list of information to be covered in a presentation and its appropriate sequence, a presentation plan allows the speaker to indicate the timing for the presentation. It also allows another speaker to conduct the same presentation effectively as all relevant information is clearly set out. A well-designed presentation plan also allows the speaker to revise the material again before the presentation and so saves a great deal of research time.

A well-designed set of notes may also be used for legal purposes should the situation ever arise.

What should a presentation plan include?

Presentation plans normally include the following:

- a session title
- presentation objectives clearly stated
- total presentation times
- participant details
- potential faults to be aware of
- review notes of the previous presentation/s
- a need for the participants to know
- method of presentation
- content of the presentation
- lists of new terms
- key questions to be asked
- resources required for the presentation
- timing for the presentation
- participant activities
- a link forward to the next presentation (if relevant).

When considering the subject matter, it is important to identify those things that the participants 'must know', 'should know' and 'could know'. The 'must know' items are those that the participants must know in order to perform the task or duty required. The 'should know' items are the things that may be needed if the student is to gain a clear understanding of the essential information. The 'could know' items are the things that may be desirable for clear understanding but are not essential.

Look at the target on page 42. Using this target, our presentation or instruction is aimed at the 'must know' area. It would be reasonable to assume that if we aimed at the bull's eye a certain amount of time would also be spent in the 'should know' area. If time permits, let the students look in the 'could know' area, but the time would probably be better spent reviewing the 'must know' and 'should know' areas. In an information-type presentation it's usually better to teach too little well, than to teach too much badly. It is up to the individual presenter to categorise information into these groups but the task is made easier if you look at the course curriculum in a formal training situation.

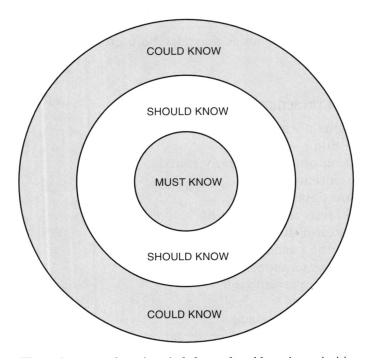

The trainer must keep in mind the students' learning priorities

A presentation plan allows you to check in advance that the sequencing is correct, that the content is relevant, and that the intended methods of presentation are suitable. The presentation plan also acts as a resource checklist for the speaker. It also allows the speaker to prepare well in advance for any material that may be required for the presentation, such as handouts, films, overhead transparencies, videos, slides, projection equipment, samples, and so on.

When writing presentation plans, one important question that should be asked in an instructional-type presentation, but which is generally overlooked is, 'What is the best way to *learn* this topic?' (Not *teach* it).

A presentation plan should, ideally, have five columns (refer to the sample shown at the end of this chapter). These should be titled:

- Timing
- Content (what information is to be given)
- Presentation technique
- Audience activity
- Presentation aids required

A well-prepared presentation plan helps the presenter to keep the instruction on target

Timing indicates the running time of the session. It allows the speaker to pace activities throughout the session and finish on time.

Content lists all of the things that have to be covered during the session. Generally key words are all that are required as memory joggers.

Presentation technique indicates whether the particular section of the session is to be of a lecture style, show and tell, or perhaps participant discovery. This is generally used only for training-type presentations.

Audience activity is a new concept for training situations. If the presenter lists the types of things that the participant will be doing during the session (listening, looking, practising, etc.) it becomes possible to build in variety in advance.

Presentation aids required is the column for the presenter to note when presentation aids are required. It is also a good idea to have all of your aids numbered so that, should they get mixed up, you can put them back into sequence or flick through them quickly to find the one needed.

Conclusion

A presentation plan is an essential piece of equipment for the presenter. It serves to guide the presentation in the correct sequence and ensures that all relevant material is covered during the presentation.

It provides a check to see if objectives are being met, if relevant. It can be checked by others to see if the presentation plan and objectives are both working in the same direction and not against each other.

It is very important that presentation plans be revised or updated by the speaker or trainer if they are going to be used on a regular basis. This should be done as soon as the presenter is aware of the need, or when changes in technology occur which affect the specific presentation.

There is no *best* format or style that may be used for a presentation plan. The best one for any presenter to use is one that is easily understood and which can be used effectively in the typical setting.

Once a presentation plan has been drafted, the best way to be sure you can improve it is to actually use it. It's surprising how many presenters, instructors or trainers leave their presentation plans in their folders and do not refer to them during the presentation.

Application example

Assume that you have been given the task of preparing a presentation on the use of a bundy machine to a group of new employees. One of the first things you would probably do is to look at the machine to become familiar with it. You would also do some research on its operation, the manufacturer, what it is used for, and many other things. When enough background information has been collected the task of writing the presentation plan can begin.

For this exercise we have to make a few assumptions. We will assume that the presentation is to last no more than fifteen minutes, that you have six participants and that you have at least one bundy machine as a sample.

It is simplest to write a presentation plan at this stage and then to modify it if necessary when you look back over it. What should the presentation plan look like after the initial research has been carried out and the information sorted?

The presentation plan shown below may be used by any presenter or trainer who has some knowledge of a bundy machine. It is easy to understand and can also be used as a reference document before presenting the session.

At the conclusion of the presentation the presenter should modify the session notes if required, making any alterations while the ideas are still fresh. If this machine becomes superseded, so do the presentation plans and new ones must be made to suit the new machine.

Further reading

Craig, Robert, *Training and Development Handbook*, 4th edn, McGraw-Hill Book Company, New York, 1996.

Field, Laurie, *Skilling Australia*, Longman Cheshire, Melbourne, 1990.

Hughes, Shirley, *Professional Presentations*, McGraw-Hill Book Company, Sydney, 1990.

Kalish, Karen, *How To Give A Terrific Presentation*, Amacom, New York, 1997.

Sample presentation plan   Sheet no. 1

Title:	How to use the bundy machine.
Written by:	Author's name_____ Date written _____
Objectives:	At the end of this session the participants will be able to: 1. state one reason for using the bundy machine 2. demonstrate the correct use of the bundy machine located in the workshop 3. state when the bundy machine is used.
Presentation time:	15 minutes
Number of participants:	6 (up to 10)
Entry level:	New employees
Aids/equipment:	• sample bundy machine • 6 bundy cards for each participant • whiteboard and markers
Potential faults:	Session not to be conducted at start or finish time of workshop.
Method:	Show and tell

Sample presentation plan				Sheet no. 2
Timing (minutes)	Content (what information is to be given)	Presentation technique	Audience activity	Presentation aids required
Introduction 0–2	Introduction • Topic • Facilitator Link back to previous session Motivator • Pay requirement	Lecture	Listening	Whiteboard
Body 2–10	Describe bundy machine and purpose	Lecture	Listening	Sample machine & cards
	How to use machine	Show & tell	Observation	Sample machine & cards
	How to fix simple problems	Show & tell	Observation	Sample machine
		Go to workshop	Practice	Machine & cards
Conclusion 10–15	Each participant to demonstrate correct use of the bundy in the workshop	Hands-on	Doing/test	Machine & cards
	Questions to group: • Give one reason for using the bundy. • When do you use the bundy? Link to next session on pay and conditions	Questions	Answering verbally	

Sample presentation plan   Sheet no. 1

Title: _____

_____

_____

Written by: _____ Date: _____

Objectives: _____

_____

_____

_____

_____

_____

_____

_____

Presentation
time: _____

Number of
participants: _____

Entry level: _____

Aids/equipment: _____

_____

_____

_____

_____

_____

_____

Potential faults: _____

_____

Method: _____

_____

Sample presentation plan				Sheet no. 2
Timing	Content (what information is to be given)	Presentation technique	Audience activity	Presentation aids required

CHAPTER 7

Methods of presentation

All presenters must realise that if the same method of instruction is used all the time, it can build a barrier to learning. For example, a presenter or trainer who uses games and role-plays all the time might have little success with that method when instructing a group in the use of a computer. Similarly, the presenter or trainer who uses the lecture technique constantly might find that it is sometimes inappropriate or that some variety is needed.

The intention here is to list fifteen different methods of instruction and then very briefly describe when or where they can be used effectively. It's important to remember that these methods are not all limited to the boardroom or the classroom. Many of them may be used outdoors or in social-type presentations. The methods to be discussed here are:

- the lecture
- a modified lecture
- the demonstration
- student practice
- student reading
- group discussion
- a fishbowl
- role-plays
- simulation
- games
- videos/films
- brainstorming
- programmed instruction
- field trips
- question and answer.

Methods

The lecture

The **lecture** is often referred to as *talking to* or *talking at* the group; it is simply addressing a passive audience. To be effective, lecturers need to be on top of things at all times and to be interesting or amusing to the audience. They also need to use an appropriate number of analogies, the correct level of language for the audience and a logical sequence of ideas in the presentation. Many institutions in our education system still use the lecture, but with this method the students cannot contribute to the learning experience. However, one significant advantage of the lecture is that the presentation time can be judged to the minute.

For a lecture to be effective, the presenter needs to be aware of the audience at all times. The presenter's voice is particularly important, both in level and tone. Also, the material must be made meaningful to the group so that they will want to listen. It is also possible, and advisable, to use presentation aids in a lecture presentation.

Unfortunately, the lecture does not generally allow for any form of immediate evaluation, or for any two-way communication between the presenter and the audience.

Modified lecture

A **modified lecture** is similar to a lecture except that the lecturer encourages some group participation. The modified lecture is now very common in adult

The lecture method of training can be very effective as long as the lecturer gives an interesting presentation

training; the lecturer often relies on participant experiences to generate some form of discussion.

The lecturer/presenter needs to make it clear from the beginning that the session is not a straight lecture and that, in fact, group discussion or participation is welcomed. Questions should also be encouraged. This form of presentation should allow for some form of evaluation at the end.

The modified lecture is an extremely efficient method of instruction and is commonly used in private training programs. When preparing for this type of presentation you will need to allow sufficient time for group participation.

The demonstration

The **demonstration** allows the participants or students to observe what the presentation is about. Most demonstrations are limited to situations requiring motor skills, such as using a bundy machine or folding a serviette. But this need not be the case. Demonstrations could also be used for showing students interpersonal skills, such as interviewing and counselling.

A demonstration should follow a planned sequence—a verbal explanation, showing the item or skill, demonstrating the skill, student questioning and student practice.

Among the things to remember when using demonstrations are that you should break the task into bite-size pieces so that the student can progress through mini-goals rather than trying to achieve everything at once. When demonstrating you must ensure that all members of the group can see the demonstration. It is also a good idea to check that all of your equipment is in working order before the demonstration (to save embarrassment). Above all, make sure that there is ample time for students to practise the skill.

For further information on skill demonstration refer to Chapter 5.

Student practice

Student practice should be allowed for after every method of instruction. It is pointless to teach someone a new skill and not encourage them to use and perfect it. It is the presenter's and trainer's responsibility to encourage trainees to apply the skill. Under supervised practice students find out whether they can use the new skill effectively or not. The trainer also finds out whether he or she has reached the final objective of the student being able to perform the skill when out of the controlled atmosphere of the training room.

Audience or student practice on-the-job is where we finally observe behavioural changes. This is the most effective form of practice and ultimately the most important evaluation.

Positive feedback to students from this exercise is also likely to encourage them to want to know more and may encourage them to undertake further instruction in the area. They learn the effectiveness of training.

Student reading

Student reading can be used effectively or it may be a total waste of everyone's time and effort. Student reading before or during a course can be extremely relevant to group discussions and exercises. However, if there are one or two participants who for some reason do not do the set reading, it may mean that they don't know what's happening if the rest of the group decides to carry on. Alternatively, the group may have to mark time while the trainer brings these people up to date with a quick overview.

Students must be given an incentive to spend their own time reading course material. The presenter could perhaps tell them that there will be a quiz for them to do. Also, they should know that if they don't do the required reading they will be wasting not only their own time but the time of the group as well. A recent idea is to give the participants note pads which have structured exercises for them to perform while reading. An example of such exercises could be a series of statements with missing words or phrases that the participant must fill in. If the presenter uses a structured note pad, many other forms of assignment can be designed for the student to undertake while reading.

Group discussion

Group discussion covers many methods of discussion and we will look at three of them briefly.

Structured discussion is a discussion between the participants to meet set objectives. It is usually better for the group to have input to the topics to be covered to meet the objective as this gives them more motivation. The motivation comes from the fact that they are basically responsible for setting the agenda.

Open forum discussion, an unstructured discussion, is basically a free-for-all with the facilitator as a go-between or referee. This type of discussion can be used to voice opinions or vent frustrations. One problem that can arise from this unstructured discussion is that the group may have one or two dominant people who tend to do all the talking. The facilitator should set ground rules before the discussion starts (or during it if necessary). One solution is to nominate an object in the room as the 'microphone'. Only the person holding the microphone may speak, and when it is passed on to someone else the new holder takes a turn.

Panel discussions are almost like a lecture in that they generally do not allow for a great deal of participant input. The panel is usually made up of a group of topic experts each with their own subtopic. The facilitator starts at a logical point and each expert builds on top of the previous expert, all of the topics being related. To be effective, this instruction method needs to be mixed with a question and answer method, or perhaps the requirement for the participants to do some preliminary work on the subject matter.

For further information on group discussion or group work refer to Chapter 8.

Fishbowl

A **fishbowl** is a description for a particular type of exercise. It is a method that can be used for analysis of group process or as a monitor to the effectiveness of group discussion.

The participants need to be seated in two circles—a small inner circle with a larger circle around it. The trainer usually selects an important, or controversial, topic and formulates several discussion-provoking questions. These questions are given to one person in the inner circle. It is the responsibility of those in the inner circle to keep the discussion going on the set topic. A number of observers are appointed to sit in the outer circle and they are asked to note things, such as who is doing all of the talking, who is interrupting, does the discussion get sidetracked very often, are there many disagreements, are there any signs of non-verbal communication and any other points the facilitator wants to include in the debriefing of the exercise. The group members should be shuffled around so that all have at least one turn in the inner circle as a participant and a turn in the outer circle as an observer.

This is obviously a fairly complicated method and it would be advisable for new trainers to avoid a fishbowl until they feel comfortable with simpler group work methods.

Role-plays

Role-plays are situational examples. A role-playing exercise normally involves the facilitator, or sometimes the group, in designing a simple script about a situation the participant may be placed in. It is then a matter of getting some of the group members to act out the situation in identified positions, using previous experience, new knowledge or skills given to them, or other methods they would like to try under controlled conditions.

Try to let the participants do most of the work because this will give them the commitment to follow the role-play through. Don't use too many props, as they may be distracting; let the group members use their imagination for the setting. Make the whole show fast-moving and try to get everyone involved. Use different players in the same situation for different ideas if needed.

It is essential that a debriefing be held as soon as the role-play exercise is finished. This gives everyone feedback on the process and highlights important points or issues raised by the group.

Simulations

Simulations are sometimes used for team-building exercises. They are not unlike role-plays but are more complex in their structure and require more participant input. With simulations, the group has to act in a team role, such as a team of consultants or a board of directors. With large groups it is advisable to break them into smaller teams with different exercises. This requires all of the team members to have an input into the exercise.

The groups are normally placed in a situation where they must get together and solve problems or build empires. It is normally a very descriptive exercise and may run for a number of months.

When the simulations have been completed, let the groups present their findings or results to all of the participants. Not only may someone pick up some good ideas, but it is also a conclusion to the exercise. In some simulations a lot of team effort is used and this presentation period is the group's opportunity to show how successful they were.

Simulations are also used for the individual trainee. Such exercises tend to be complex and generally expensive to set up. Examples of those involving an individual trainee may be flight simulators and driving simulators.

Games

Games can be simple (joining the dots in the shortest time) or very complex (who can show a million dollar profit first?). Games are normally competitive and usually relate directly to the task involved.

5   9   7   2
  12   23   6
3   13   25

A wide variety of interesting, competitive games can be used in training situations

If games are made to be competitive, they should not identify winners and losers but should identify a variety of thoughts and ideas and show how others may use them.

When games are used to develop or improve skills, they can be used at any stage during the course. Experienced trainers tend to keep their games for use after breaks. If you find a lively game that gets everyone involved and moving around, it may be worth designing your session so that this game can be used immediately after lunch.

There are many books now available that contain hundreds of proven games for different topics. If you design your own games and they are successful, share them with other trainers.

For more information on games, simulations and role-plays see Chapter 9.

Videos and films

Videos or **films** may generally be used as support for the presenter but should not be used as the sole method of instruction. If trainees have difficulties with the material or have questions to be answered, they need someone to talk to.

Videos and films are usually used to reinforce the main points of the presenter's presentation. It may be desirable to use a video or film occasionally as a change of pace. If videos or films are used to support the presentation they must be introduced to the group and the group be made aware of what to look for. At the conclusion, the presenter must review the ideas and material covered and clarify any points that may not have been understood.

The presenter must preview any video or film before it is used. Check that it is relevant, covers the points required and make sure that it isn't out of date.

A presentation should not be designed around the film content—the film should fit into the previously designed session. The film should complement the session.

Brainstorming

Brainstorming, a form of structured discussion, is a method of instruction that is not used to its full extent. It has the advantage of using the participants own thoughts, which leads to more ideas and greater participant motivation.

The presenter must first introduce a topic or problem to the group and then it is up to the participants to give as many ideas or thoughts as possible. All ideas must be positive, no negative ideas are allowed. They are listed on a whiteboard or flip chart but not discussed straight away. The object is to get as many ideas as possible and it doesn't matter how absurd they are (ridiculous ideas are encouraged). When the group has been exhausted of ideas then you can go back and start discussing each idea. The group then decides which idea/s are best suited to the problem and applies the results.

Brainstorming with a group gives more, and generally better, ideas than an individual is able to provide. This is called synergy—the total is greater than the sum of the parts.

Programmed instruction

Programmed instruction (computer-based instruction) is not a new idea but is now becoming more recognised through the use of computers.

Trainees can proceed at their own pace with programmed instruction

The concept of programmed instruction is to break a task into as many segments as possible. Each segment has to be mastered by trainees before they are allowed to progress to the next section. If they are unable to answer questions on a section correctly they are given more exercises to perform until the section has been mastered.

With this method of instruction trainees must have an input to the learning process—if they don't participate, nothing happens. When the trainees are participating their efforts are acknowledged, whether they are right or wrong.

Programmed instruction may be used for any topic, from playing chess, to reading skills, to flying a plane. It's easy to see how computers are now being used in programmed instruction as they can give the trainee more and more exercises, or speed up to suit the faster, or more knowledgeable, learner.

Field trips

Field trips may be useful if they have been thought out properly. If we intend taking our trainees on some sort of excursion or tour it must be planned. The trip must be meaningful to the trainees and they must be motivated to want to attend.

When we plan our field trip we are designing a complete session. The only difference is that the session isn't being conducted totally in the classroom. The design of the session will include a clearly stated objective, a need for the trainees to be attentive, an introduction to the exercise, a body (the trip itself), a conclusion (or debrief), and some form of evaluation.

A well-planned field trip, with associated exercises for the trainees, can be a useful training method

A popular method now used for field trips is to give the trainees a number of exercises or observations to be carried out before the conclusion of the trip. This concept can be used for any form of field trip, including visits to other offices.

Question and answer techniques

Question and answer techniques are now employed in most classrooms. The question and answer technique can be given a title of modified discussion. It involves some trainee participation and gives the presenter or trainer a good indication of whether the message is being received or not. It may indicate that some areas need to be revised or revisited.

The presenter should ask questions of the group often, making sure that they are relevant to the topic. The questions must be spread around the group so that all of the trainees are participating. If people are having trouble answering the question, don't give them the answer. You can rephrase the question, prompt them, give them clues or get someone else in the group to assist them.

Conclusion

A presentation should not rely on a sole method of instruction for all subjects. The experienced presenter will be able to look at a topic and decide on a number of methods that can be used independently, or combined, for maximum benefit to the learner.

The presenter must make the decision on which method to use based on the learners' requirements, not on what the presenter feels like doing. It has been found that most participants want to have some form of input to the learning exercise, so the presenter should consider using the participants' knowledge in the session design and the methods selected.

A well-structured course would have more than one method of instruction in its design. Remember that variety is necessary, but don't go overboard.

Application example

What works for one presenter may not necessarily work for another. As most people use different methods of instruction, there will not be an application example for this chapter. However, as an exercise you can think of a subject that you haven't presented before. With this subject in mind, try to see from the learner's point of view some methods that may get the message across in a non-threatening way. If you can't think of a subject, try something such as law or office procedures.

When you have done this, apply the same idea to something you are instructing in now. Are you surprised that you may have seen it differently from the learner's point of view? It may be time to modify some of your session plans to incorporate other methods of instruction.

An interesting session I once participated in was a legal presentation on the area of omission and commission. It started with a group of people carrying in a corpse (fake) on a table covered with a sheet. The staff became the main role-players with the audience playing the part of the jury. Without going into great detail I think that you can see that a strong learning atmosphere was created from a relatively boring subject.

The new presenter has to start somewhere, so you will probably use other presenters ideas to begin with. These ideas may or may not be right and they may or may not suit you. Once you have used them you must modify them to suit your own style.

Further reading

Baird, L., Schneier, C. & Laird, D., *The Training and Development Sourcebook*, 2nd edn, Human Resource Press, Massachusetts, 1994.

Kroehnert, Gary, *100 Training Games*, McGraw-Hill Book Company, Sydney, 1991.

Laird, Dugan, *Approaches to Training and Development*, 2nd edn, Addison-Wesley Publishing Company, Massachusetts, 1985.

Mill, Cyril, *Activities for Trainers: 50 Useful Designs*, University Associates, California, 1980.

Newstrom, J. W. & Scannell, E. E., *Games Trainers Play*, McGraw-Hill Book Company, New York, 1980.

Scannell, E. E. & Newstrom, J. W., *More Games Trainers Play*, McGraw-Hill Book Company, New York, 1983.

Zemke, R. & Kramlinger, T., *Figuring Things Out: A Trainers Guide to Needs and Task Analysis*, Addison-Wesley Publishing Company, Massachusetts, 1981, Chapter 18.

CHAPTER 8

Group methods

This chapter looks closely at one of the methods of instruction described in the previous chapter. It deals specifically with the techniques and purposes of group sessions and group work, as used in workshops, seminars, conferences and social-type presentations. The main ideas are basically the same regardless of which setting they are used in. We will also look at some suggestions for effective use of these methods.

What are group methods?

Group methods describe a number of activities including games, simulations, role-playing, team-building exercises and brainstorming. In group methods we also include some group techniques, such as the Nominal group process, DACUM, Critical incident technique and the Delphi technique. Group methods can best be described as a process of ideas and roles between individuals in a group setting.

Ideas and *roles* are the two main issues involved with a group. There must be a leader so that the group is guided to achieve its objective—the task it was brought together for in the first place. However, as well as achieving that objective, the group is involved in the process of getting the task done. Ideally, there should be a balance between the task and the process.

Historically, new presenters or trainers are mainly concerned about getting the group to perform the task. Experienced presenters and trainers are more likely to be concerned with how the performance was designed or processed, in addition to the ultimate outcome.

In many group meetings the group leader wants to get something done, but does not care about how the outcome is reached. On the other hand, some group leaders can see that the process may be just as important as the outcome. They still get the job done and tend to get the job done more effectively because the group feels motivated to carry it out properly.

What types of groups are there?

As presenters, trainers or facilitators we probably deal with five separate types of groups or meetings. These five are:

- group discussions
- conferences
- seminars
- workshops
- clinics.

There are a number of other types of groups or meetings we could consider but they tend not to be relevant to training situations. Before we carry on it may be of benefit to look at a quick outline of the five groups.

Group discussions normally involve groups of five to twenty people with common interests in the subject area. They are conversational-style discussions where all of the individual members have equal rights and access to the subject. A group discussion must be under the control of a trained facilitator or group leader. The group leader must remain impartial in discussion but ensure that the group stays on the topic and that all participants do, in fact, have equal input.

Conferences usually involve larger groups. The numbers may vary from five to five thousand or more. The participants normally represent different departments or organisations, but all have a common interest or background.

Some conferences are simply venues for participants to exchange ideas or information

The activity of a conference is usually to look at problems within a specified subject area and endeavour to arrive at solutions to them by the end of the conference time. Some conferences are simply venues for participants to exchange ideas or information, or to find out about new technology in the industry that they represent.

Seminars involve groups of any size, again from five to five thousand or more, and are conducted for a group of people who have a common need. Seminars are normally led by an expert in a topic area. In this form of group method, a problem may be defined and then given to the participants to rectify, under the supervision of the seminar leader. The seminar leader may also present relevant research findings so that the participants can discover the correct solutions based on those findings.

Seminars usually begin with a presentation by an expert before small groups
are formed for discussion

Workshops may involve groups of any size, but again the group would have a common interest or a common background. A workshop is generally conducted so that the participants can improve their ability or understanding by combining study and discussion. Workshops tend to be user-driven, that is, the participants may influence the direction of the program at its very beginning. In a workshop attendees are generally prepared for a hands-on type presentation.

Clinics are meetings where a small group of people with common interests examine a real-life problem. The group members diagnose and analyse the problem and then offer solutions. Clinics may be used to establish procedures as they are based on real-life situations and the participants generally offer working solutions based on their past experiences.

What are the group techniques?

The four group techniques we will look at include the Nominal group process, DACUM, Critical incident technique and the Delphi technique.

The **Nominal group process** involves a group of people who meet to solve a problem described to them by the group leader. In silence and to the clock, the group members must write down a number of their individual responses or ideas. The group leader then takes one idea at a time and lists them all on a chart or board. If explanation or clarification is needed, it is provided by the originator of the idea after all of the ideas have been collected from the group. After all ideas have been listed, the group members must individually rank the responses. The group leader takes these individual rankings and processes them to give the final rankings of the combined group.

One possible problem with this technique is that it doesn't draw on facts. However, this may be offset by the time efficiency of the whole process.

DACUM (Develop A CurriculUM) is normally used by training staff to develop a curriculum and is achieved by dissecting a position into jobs and

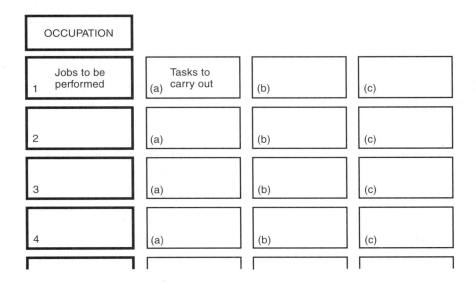

DACUM, one of the group techniques, involves dissecting a position into various jobs and tasks

tasks. A group of ten to fifteen experts (usually supervisors or skilled workers) set aside a period of time at a venue free from distractions. The group leader is responsible for having an occupation or position dissected so that a curriculum can be designed to meet the exact training needs of the employee.

This technique may also be used to establish varying levels of competency by the employee—that is, basic levels, intermediate levels and advanced levels of knowledge or skill proficiency.

The **Critical incident technique** involves having each individual in a group identify the critical incidents which lead to the problem or situation that has been described. When all of the incidents have been collected, they are collated and then discussed by the group. The individuals in this group must have a common interest or background in the subject matter. This technique is sometimes used in management training to get the participants to identify critical incidents in their career. It may also be used for such things as finding out what critical incidents cause the photocopier to jam up.

The **Delphi technique** is a group technique where the group members don't need to get together. It may be called the group you have when you're not having a group. It works like this. A problem or situation is identified by a management or decision-making team. A group leader is asked to identify a number of experts within the subject area. With these experts identified the group leader develops and distributes a questionnaire based on the problem or situation. When the responses have been processed the group leader then develops and distributes a second questionnaire modified to suit the previous responses. The second and subsequent questionnaires ask the respondents to reconsider their ideas based on new or composite opinions. The process may finish with the second questionnaire or continue until the group of experts reaches consensus on the suggested outcome. With consensus reached it is then up to the group leader to report the findings back to the management team.

This technique may be modified for use with an assembled group. If it is your intention to use the group in this manner it is suggested that a lot more study be carried out on the techniques involved.

Advantages and disadvantages of group techniques

As all of these group techniques have their own advantages and disadvantages (see table), it is possible to identify areas where they may be applied. Presenters or trainers may apply all of them in a training needs analysis.

It's not expected that new trainers will be 'thrown in the deep end' without some form of assistance. Should the new presenter or trainer be required to facilitate any of these group techniques, they would need to conduct much more research; the information presented here is only an overview.

The success of all group work depends heavily on the amount and quality of planning and preparation carried out in advance. You may find it worthwhile contacting the participants before any group meeting to advise them of the problem or situation. This may lead to additional ideas being generated as they have been given some thinking time beforehand.

Technique	Advantages	Disadvantages
Nominal group process	Can create group motivation Everyone participates Incorporates brainstorming Generates ideas Opportunity for discussion	Can easily become boring Cost of not having experts at work Effect on productivity with experts gone Threatening if not enough ideas to list Embarrassment by lack of ideas
DACUM	No room for error Incorporates brainstorming Cost effective Good representation of staff Generates specific information	Time consuming Tense to tiring Needs competent leader Can get bogged down in detail May miss attitudinal changes needed
Critical incident	Directly task related Input from participants Not always negative incidents Establishes correct procedures Looks at the entire situation	Time consuming and cumbersome Defining what is and isn't critical Only critical incidents are recorded Input restricted to memories Needs competent leader
Delphi	Selective participation Geographically unrestricted Respondents are isolated Groups can be large Confidentiality	Long duration Lack of ongoing interest No personal contact Unpredictable response rate Data can be lost

Conclusion

It can be seen that the new presenter or trainer needs to know the basics of group methods and group techniques. This chapter has provided an overview. Very importantly, there is a process within all groups, which is not investigated here, and would be considered an advanced level of knowledge for presenters and trainers. As new presenters and trainers gain experience with groups, they will begin to notice these processes, and will then be able to influence the group in the desired direction if needed.

It may be of interest to note that all of the group techniques we have looked at (with the exception of nominal group techniques) stipulate that the participants should have a common interest or background in the subject matter. If this common interest is missing, you may find it almost impossible to reach your objectives. However, it isn't necessary for the individuals in a nominal group process to have a common interest or background in the subject matter because the aim might be to find new ideas or solutions. Someone without an in-depth knowledge of the problem or situation may be able to offer the best solution based on their outside expertise or ideas.

Application example

An application example wouldn't be practical for this chapter, so instead I will give you some tips for starting and maintaining group discussion.

- Select a topic that everyone can become involved in.
- Let the group set ground rules for everyone to follow.
- Acknowledge all input from the participants.
- Select as your first speaker the one who will give a model answer.
- Go around the circle to begin with.
- Don't leave the suspected worst responses to last.
- Ensure that everyone gets a chance to participate.
- Always get clarification if needed.
- Look for non-verbal responses.
- Use first names and direct eye contact with the group.
- Don't always give the answers, let the group do it.
- Plant seeds so that the group may develop their own ideas.
- Move from the foreground to the background as the discussion proceeds.
- Intervene if necessary and keep the group on track.
- Be aware of your non-verbal communication.
- Be honest and enthusiastic with the group at all times. If you're not, you can bet they won't be.

Further reading

Craig, Robert, *Training and Development Handbook*, 4th edn, McGraw-Hill Book Company, New York, 1996.

Daniels, William, *Group Power One: A Manager's Guide to Using Task-force Meetings*, University Associates, California, 1986.

Heerman, Barry, *Building Team Spirit*, McGraw-Hill Book Company, New York, 1997.

Laird, Dugan, *Approaches to Training and Development*, 2nd edn, Addison-Wesley Publishing Company, Massachusetts, 1985.

Romig, Dennis A, *Breakthrough Teamwork*, Irwin Professional Publishing, Chicago, 1996.

CHAPTER 9

Games, simulations and role-plays

We have all seen and probably participated in training games, simulations and role-plays. Just because we are aware of them, does this mean that we can use them anytime we feel like it? No, it doesn't.

What we will be doing now is looking at the differences between games, simulations and role-plays. We will consider when it may be appropriate to use them and we will look at a brief example of each.

The use of games, simulations and role-plays allows the participant to discover outcomes, rather than to be told everything without trying it. Most of the world's airlines, manufacturing plants, human resource companies, military establishments, small and large companies, and private and public organisations now use games, simulations and role-plays in training. The ultimate outcome of using games, simulations and role-plays is improved learning.

What is the difference?

A game

A game is an activity, illustration or exercise that can support the point the presenter, trainer or facilitator is trying to get across to the audience or

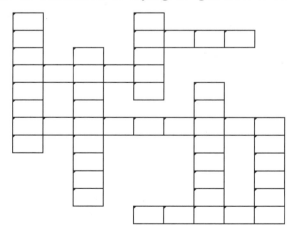

The use of games in training helps the participants to discover the outcome of actions for themselves

trainees. A game is normally brief, is not felt as threatening by the participants, requires all the participants to participate, is not complicated, is inexpensive, generally contains one learning point, is predictable in its results and is generally adaptable to a wide variety of situations.

A game may not always appear to have any direct relevance to the topic. It may only be when the experience is discussed later that the participant sees the relevance or the point the presenter wanted to make. If this discussion does not take place the attendees may never see any connection between the game and the subject matter, and the whole exercise is wasted.

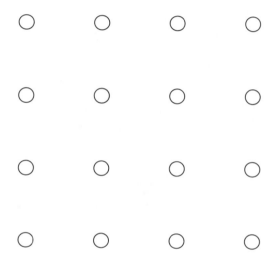

Can you join the 16 dots with six straight continuous lines?
(You are not allowed to lift your pencil off the paper or retrace your path.)

Games are an ideal way to provide activity, but their contribution to learning must be made clear too

A simulation

A simulation is usually more complex than a game in its design. Simulations are the presenters mock-up of the real thing. They can range from a simple paper mock-up of utensils or furniture, to exact replicas of the inside of a motor vehicle or aircraft using sophisticated computers to run them. The cost of these simulators can range from a few dollars to many millions of dollars. Even if they only cost a couple of dollars though, you will generally find that they require a lot of the presenter's preparation time.

The use of a simulation allows the participant to try new behaviours without endangering the real product or suffering terrible consequences if something goes wrong.

Simulation exercises can be very instructive

A role-play

A role-play is similar to a simulation except that it doesn't use any props. Normally, the only items required for a role-play are a script or an idea, and one or more participants. The situations that the participants act out are usually related to the workplace and involve situations that the players might be involved in. After the role-players have been identified, they act out the parts as they would normally, or perhaps try new behaviours shown to them during the presentation or during the training. Once the scenario has been played out, the role-players, the rest of the group and the presenter carry out a critique of the role-play. They identify good and bad points, include suggestions for other behaviours and suggest any other possibilities.

Role-plays are normally followed by group discussion, and time must be allowed for this very important part of the session.

Role-playing is a vivid way of learning how to handle on-the-job situations

When can we use these techniques?

For most of us, games, simulations and role-plays were part of the process of growing up. Right back to our earliest recollections of school days, we remember playing games such as marbles or hide-and-seek. It is now recognised that these games not only provide fun but also prepare the child for entry into the social system. If any of you took Home Economics, Woodwork or Metalwork at school you would probably call them a simulation of the real workplace. Some of us may also remember when we acted out roles in a game of 'Mothers and Fathers', another form of role-play. We can actually trace the use of games and simulations back thousands of years. Chess is an example of this. It was developed by the military and was based on solving military problems.

In a presentation or training situation we must be very selective in the use and timing of these methods of instruction. People become bored doing the same thing all the time, even if it is a 'mind-blowing experience' the first few times. If you intend using these methods effectively, plan them into your session notes or outline. This is one situation where we definitely need to apply the principles of adult learning (review the nine principles in Chapter 1).

So when can you use these techniques? They may be used any time as long as you feel that using a game, simulation or role-play would be the most effective way for the participants to learn what they are intended to learn or discover. Don't just use them for the sake of variety.

You can, however, use games or drills as a means of channelling excess energy or to liven up the class. The activity can be a means of improving the learning atmosphere. So games or drills should be selected and used on the basis of their usefulness, for reinforcing the instruction, or improving the learning environment.

| Samples

A game

A simple type of game for part of a presentation or trainer training course might be to see who can draw the straightest line on the whiteboard, the winner receiving a new whiteboard marker. This type of game is simple, non-threatening, has no losers and is inexpensive.

Discussion later would highlight the main purpose behind the game. This might be to let the trainees see that it's not as easy as it looks to draw a straight line on the whiteboard. The game could also motivate some of the trainees to improve their techniques on the whiteboard through practice.

A simulation

We have probably all seen a tennis serving machine before. If you haven't, it's a machine which is set up on one side of a tennis court and 'serves' tennis balls out at different speeds and angles. Wouldn't you agree that this is a simulation? Wouldn't you also agree that using this serving machine is easier to organise than trying to get a group of tennis players for your trainee to practice with? Using this type of equipment would also allow for a greater variation of 'players' anyway.

After the training session using the machine, we would have a debriefing period which would give suggestions to improve bad returns. If the trainee encounters a large number of bad returns, they won't continuously lose the game using this type of simulation. Imagine how hard it would be to want to try to improve yourself if you kept on losing 'real' matches.

A role-play

If we were training welfare workers, wouldn't it be fair to assume that we would want them to counsel someone as part of their training? Of course we would. Wouldn't it also be fair to assume that we couldn't just go out onto the street to find volunteers? Right again. This is where the role-play comes in. We would probably describe a scenario to the group and then ask a couple of the participants to come forward and act it out. After they had completed that task, and we had discussed the effects, we could then break the group into smaller groups and get all of them to role-play other similar situations. The concluding discussion should involve ideas for improvements, based on the role-playing experience.

Conclusion

Gone are the days when games and the like were not considered to be suitable as presentation or training methods. The presentation of information or training is a serious business, but we can and should use games or simulations in these situations.

War games (simulations) have been used by military personnel for many, many centuries and have proved to be very effective. Games, simulations and role-plays are relatively new to training and are proving to be very effective, if used properly.

Regardless of how good we are as presenters or lecturers, we can't fool ourselves into thinking that our presentation alone is going to keep everyone's interest for the whole period. The use of a game or simulation is an application of the principles of adult learning. Be sure that the participants do not become over-involved in the game or simulation and thus actually miss the learning point. Also, if the participants have too high a level of enthusiasm for the game or simulation, they may become bored with normal training.

The learning process can be speeded up by the use of games, simulations and role-plays. It is well known that people learn better when they are enjoying themselves. So we should seriously think about creating or supplying the appropriate learning atmosphere.

We should always select the presentation method or training method after we have set the objectives and it should respond to the trainees' needs, and not the presenter's or trainer's needs.

When we decide to start using a game, simulation or role-play, it is important that we practise the exercise at least once with a group of people not involved in the immediate presentation. This helps the presenter or trainer to see if the design is going to work, and in the expected way. Like all types of training, games, simulations and role-plays must be evaluated for their worth and effectiveness. If they don't produce what is needed, scrap or modify them.

The inventive presenter can design new forms of familiar games to provide variety

Application example

An application example for this chapter would serve little purpose. All it would do is give you another example of a game, simulation or role-play. What I would suggest now is that you read about a number of games, simulations and role-plays. Three of the texts listed at the end of this chapter contain hundreds of examples. The texts are:

- *100 Training Games*
- *Activities for Trainers: 50 Useful Designs*
- *Games Trainers Play*

Read as many texts as you feel comfortable with; these three are fun. Use your imagination to see where you could use them. When we talk about designing new games or simulations, it is normally a matter of modifying an existing design to suit new conditions. Totally new games or simulations are very rare.

Further reading

Bishop, Sue, *Training Games for Assertiveness and Conflict Resolution*, McGraw-Hill Book Company, New York, 1997.

Burnard, Philip, *Training Games for Interpersonal Skills*, McGraw-Hill Book Company, New York, 1994.

Craig, Robert, *Training and Development Handbook*, 4th edn, McGraw-Hill Book Company, New York, 1996.

Elgood, Chris, *Handbook of Management Games*, 5th edn, Gower Publishing Company, England, 1993.

Forbess-Greene, Sue, T*he Encyclopedia of Icebreakers*, University Associates, California, 1983.

Heerman, Barry, *Building Team Spirit*, McGraw-Hill Book Company, New York, 1997.

Kirk, James & Kirk, Lynne, *Training Games for the Learning Organisation*, McGraw-Hill Book Company, New York, 1997.

Kroehnert, Gary, *100 Training Games*, McGraw-Hill Book Company Sydney, 1992.

Mill, Cyril, *Activities for Trainers: 50 Useful Designs*, University Associates, California, 1980.

Newstrom, J. W. & Scannell, E. E., *Games Trainers Play*, McGraw-Hill Book Company, New York, 1980.

Rogers, Jennifer, *Adults Learning*, 2nd edn, Open University Press, England, 1979, Chapter 8.

Romig, Dennis A., *Breakthrough Teamwork*, Irwin Professional Publishing, Chicago, 1996.

Scannell, E. E. & Newstrom, J. W., *More Games Trainers Play*, McGraw-Hill Book Company, New York, 1983.

Turner, David, *60 Role Plays for Management and Supervisory Training*, McGraw-Hill Book Company, New York, 1996.

CHAPTER 10

Presenter effectiveness

This chapter will deal with presenter or trainer effectiveness or what we should look for in a good presenter or trainer. Fortunately, all presenters and trainers are not the same as each other, so this chapter is looking at a base level of skills which the new presenter or trainer can develop and build on.

The presenter's appearance

A presenter should look like a professional. But how is that achieved? Firstly, the person giving the presentation should dress according to the type of instruction being given, and who it's being given to.

If you are going to instruct resuscitation techniques to swimmers at a swimming pool, you could safely assume that you don't have to wear your Sunday best. On the other hand, if you're going to give a presentation to a group of senior managers in resuscitation techniques in a boardroom, you certainly wouldn't be wearing shorts, singlet and sneakers. Ideally, you shouldn't stand out from the crowd, but you should keep your dress standards higher than the rest of the group.

The presenter should also look organised. If you're going into a classroom, boardroom or lecture theatre, have all your material in a neat and organised pile with the things you want to use first on top and then work down into the stack.

Have you ever noticed how some presenters or trainers carry everything they could possibly ever need, but only use a small percentage of it? If you're going to carry all this material, at least have it organised so that you can find things quickly if you need them.

Where should the presenter stand?

If you are going to stand as you present the session, you should be standing in front of the group (looks a bit silly standing at the back). However, if you stand too still you can lose the group's attention. Move around a little, but not too much, just enough to keep the participants watching you.

Don't try to hide yourself behind the chair, desk, lectern or overhead projector. This can create a barrier to your communication and therefore to learning. Stand in front or to the side of any equipment so that the participants can see all of you if they want to.

If you do stand in front of your presentation aids, you must ensure that everyone in the group can see around you. If they can't, your body has become a physical and mental barrier to learning. Also, they may not let you know that you are obscuring their view, so it is up to you to notice.

If you're sitting in front of the group the same principles apply. Allow the group to see all of you. It shows the group that you're open to them and not hiding anything from them.

Communicating with attendees

A lot has been said over the years about the presenter's or trainer's mannerisms. Some of these mannerisms may be verbal ones, such as 'umm', 'errh' and 'you know'. Other types of mannerisms may be rubbing a nose, scratching a neck, fiddling with bits of paper, fiddling with pens, looking at notes constantly or trying to crush a whiteboard marker.

If the presenter or the trainer is using many different types of instructional methods, his or her mannerisms probably aren't too distracting. It's normally only if the presenter or the trainer spends a long period of time with a group that any mannerisms need to be thought about and a remedy found. Usually the more presentation experience we have, the fewer our distracting mannerisms.

A good presenter can read the audience's body language. By looking at the participants faces you can usually tell if they do not understand what the instruction is about. You must also be aware that the audience can read your body language, so don't stand in front of the group with your arms folded and tell them that you're open to questions (unless you want to go home early).

It's important for the presenter not to interrupt a participant who is talking. A participant who is cut off may tend to keep quiet after that insult. Obviously, there are times when you do have to cut short a participant who talks too much. If you don't, it can interfere with your communication to the whole group.

For effective communication to continue, the presenter must offer positive reinforcement to the participants during the session. This means acknowledging responses from the group to encourage more interaction. If you ignore any responses, you are likely to lose interaction. Sometimes a particular member may stop contributing after being ignored, even if they have the information you're after.

Presenters must be lively, enthusiastic and full of vitality. If we can display these qualities, it motivates the group to want to learn. If the participant is not motivated or interested in the instruction, learning may be very difficult, if not impossible.

Communication does not have to mean verbal communication 100 per cent of the time. Silent pauses during the instruction allow the main points to sink in. So you could plan to have some silent breaks during instruction immediately after the main points.

How should the presenter gain attention?

Humour may be used occasionally to gain the audience attention. When humour is used the presenter must be certain that it is effective and appropriate. Have you seen a presenter try to use humour to gain attention but lose the group's interest with a joke that didn't quite work?

The presenter must make certain that the topic of the joke is relevant to the topic and that the story is not too long as this can distract the participants. Humour must never be directed at any of the audience, must never use religion, must not refer to any nationality and must never be directed specifically at one sex. These censorship rules ensure that no one in the group is offended. If you offend one person in the audience the whole group may close ranks against you.

To gain, and keep, the participants' attention we need to use a variety of methods in our instruction. This means that we should use appropriate and relevant presentation aids where they fit into the session. We must also keep the participants active and involved in the session (refer to Chapters 7, 8 and 9).

Presenters should vary the pitch of their voice occasionally and volume and pace to keep the participants' attention.

By asking questions of the group we can be reasonably certain that we are gaining the participants' attention. If questions are being asked no one wants to be the one who doesn't know the answer, so use it to your advantage.

With this motivating technique we need to follow a few rules. Keep the questions short and spread them around the group. Use 'overhead' type questions, that is, ask a question of the group, wait for a few seconds, and then nominate the participant who is to answer. This technique is sometimes referred to as the 'pose, pause and pounce' method of questioning. Remember to give the participant praise for a correct answer. If you get an incorrect answer, get the group to help bring out the right answer.

Creating interest

If visual aids are used by the presenter or trainer they must be made to attract and keep the participants' interest. When you put notes or phrases on overhead transparencies or on the whiteboard you should make them *mean* something.

By writing legibly and neatly on the whiteboard you can keep the participants' interest. If the writing is untidy or difficult to understand the audience may just give up. If you're an untidy writer on the whiteboard, chalkboard or flip chart, take some time to practise so that you can improve your style.

To create interest you can always link new material back to something the audience is familiar with—relating new knowledge to previous knowledge.

Wherever possible the presenter or trainer should show that all of the subject matter relates to real life situations. If the audience can see that the information may be of benefit to them, the presenter is creating interest.

A couple of other things that will make it more interesting for the participants are the use of curiosity and the use of competition. It may be difficult to make the audience curious about your subject but think about it and then try it. A sense of competition can also provoke interest, but the participants should not be in direct competition with each other. They should be competing with themselves by trying to improve on their own previous performance.

Good habits

Good presenters and good trainers should clean as they go. Before moving on to a new area in the session, clean the whiteboard of old material and remove any other distractions such as samples or other presentation aids. Clean up the classroom before leaving too. This will gain you some professional respect from the presenters or trainers in following sessions.

A good presenter should also start and finish on time. How do you feel when you're sitting in a room fifteen minutes after the session was supposed to start and the presenter hasn't shown up? How do you feel when the session is still in progress as your train is pulling out of the station?

A good presenter is also thoroughly prepared. This means having your objectives clearly stated, having the appropriate presentation methods selected, having a session plan and presentation aids prepared, and knowing where the spares are if anything burns out.

Conclusion

A well-prepared presenter or trainer can increase the learning success rate for the participant if he or she thinks a little about it. By looking at yourself from the participants' point of view, you may wish to change a few things.

Look at your physical appearance. Do you look like a professional public speaker or educator? Think about where you're standing when you're in front of the group. Can everyone see you? Can everyone see your presentation aids? Do you look approachable or do you look threatening?

You must be enthusiastic about your material. If you're not enthusiastic about it the audience certainly won't be. Make the communication two-way and continuous. Reward your audience when they get it right.

Vary your methods of presentation to keep the participants interested. You need to be observing your audience continually, ready to regain their attention should it start to wander off.

Your participants won't learn just by being exposed to information. It's up to you as a professional public speaker or educator to encourage active learning and to create a learning atmosphere.

Application example

If you think back to the many presentation sessions you have been involved in as a participant, which do you recall? We all tend to recall the very good presentations and the very bad presentations. This tells us as presenters that if we leave a lasting impression on our audience it will be because we fell into one of these categories. Presumably you would choose to make that the very good presentation category.

As you recall the best presentation you've sat in on, write down all of the good things you liked about it. When you've finished that list, write down all of the very bad things that you remember of the poorest presentation you have seen (you may need to think back to school days).

You can now use this list of good and bad points as a model and guide. The new presenter needs to start somewhere, so why not start with the best?

You will find that if you apply the good points on this list, you're certain to improve your style quite dramatically. If you ignore them, it may take a while for you to get from the bad side to the good side. Even experienced presenters and trainers need to sit down and look at their styles occasionally. It is easy to slip back into some bad habits and the participants generally don't tell us, do they?

Further reading

Baird, L., Schneier, C. & Laird, D., *The Training and Development Sourcebook*, 2nd edn, Human Resource Press, Massachusetts, 1994.

Hughes, Shirley, *Professional Presentations*, McGraw-Hill Book Company, Sydney, 1990.

Kalish, Karen, *How To Give A Terrific Presentation*, Amacom, New York, 1997.

Laird, Dugan, *Approaches to Training and Development*, 2nd edn, Addison-Wesley Publishing Company, Massachusetts, 1985.

There hasn't been a lot of information written specifically on this subject. Most training and development books have some material scattered through them, so keep your eyes open. Books written for public speaking techniques sometimes have information on this topic as well.

Good trainers are/do:	*Bad trainers are/do:*

CHAPTER 11

Questioning

Questions are used constantly—without them we would have very little communication. When we think about it, nearly half of what we say or use in general conversation is a question. We pose a question and get a response, then another question is directed at us and we respond, and so on.

This chapter will be looking at the types of questions we use in our presentations. As you read it, you will probably find that the information ties in with your knowledge of questions from everyday conversation.

I have no answers, only questions.
Socrates c. 300 BC

Why do we use questions?

There are many reasons for presenters and trainers using questions in a presentation or training situation. Most of the reasons are covered in this book but they are mixed through the readings. To make it easier, let's list the main reasons:

- to find out if there is a presentation or training need
- to find the entry level of participants
- to check participant recall
- to find facts
- to assist retention
- to create overlearning
- to involve the participants
- to create active learning
- to gain feedback
- to solve problems
- to check understanding
- to clarify relationships
- to use for revision
- to create discussion
- to keep participants interested
- to stimulate thought

- to redirect discussion
- to draw on participant experience.

Presenters who don't use questions are missing out on a lot of information and assistance. Without the use of questions they risk failure from the very beginning.

Types of questions

The types of questions that can be asked can be grouped in separate categories. We will now look at the main categories briefly and see where each may be used.

Direct questions

Direct questions are questions which are posed to a certain person in the group. They're not ambiguous and are usually designed to bring out the facts. The major problem when using this technique constantly is that it requires only one person to think of a response:

- 'Fred, what are the nine principles of learning?'

Such questions may be used to check an individual's understanding of the subject matter. Additionally, they may be used to redirect the group if discussion becomes sidetracked, or to involve a daydreamer in the learning process.

Overhead questions

Overhead questions are questions that we pose to the whole group, without directing the question at anyone in particular:

- 'How can we apply this technique in the workplace?' (directed at the whole group).

Overhead questions are used to check group understanding. If no-one in the group volunteers an answer, you may have to rephrase the question or give a clue to the answer.

Alternatively, you can change the question into a direct question by nominating someone to answer it, using the 'pose, pause and pounce' technique:

- 'How can we apply this technique in the workplace?' (pause) 'Fred?'

This type of questioning is probably the most effective for the new presenter to use.

Closed questions

Closed questions usually require a yes/no answer or a single word response. They're quick but don't give much accuracy if the presenter wants to check knowledge. If you use closed questions, it's sometimes advisable to follow them with a 'what, when, who, where or how' question to check the participants' knowledge further:

- Facilitator: 'Should we always use sessions plans?'

Participant: 'Yes'

Facilitator: 'How?'

Leading questions

Leading questions may be used to get explicit answers. Generally, a full description of the situation is given, followed by a question on the subject matter. This question can also include a clue to the answer:

- 'Let's imagine that you're standing in front of a class and they all appear to be restless. Which of the nine principles of learning could you apply to settle the group down? The nine principles are still shown on the whiteboard.'

This type of question calls for a very specific answer. It may be used as a direct or overhead question and it should be thought-provoking to check the participants' understanding of the material.

Rhetorical questions

Rhetorical questions are questions that don't require answers. But what good is a question without an answer? Rhetorical questions are normally used to get the audience thinking. It's not uncommon for presenters to begin their sessions by posing a rhetorical question to the group:

- 'What is testing?'

When you pose a rhetorical question to a group, don't pause too long after it or someone will start to answer and that defeats the purpose. The purpose of a rhetorical question is to get the group thinking about the subject matter.

Open-ended questions

Open-ended questions request more information of the participant and normally require more time to answer. They usually start with a 'what, when, who, where or how'. Try to avoid questions starting with 'why' as 'why' questions tend to be too broad in their interpretation. It is commonly accepted that the 'why' is an umbrella for the more specific 'what, when, who, where or how'.

- 'What do you feel is necessary to accomplish this?'

The answers to open-ended questions may show that the presenter or trainer needs to jump in quickly to redirect the response to the required area of thinking. Sometimes open-ended questions can be used to start group discussion.

Effective questions

An effective question should be designed with the following in mind:
- it should be short
- it should have only one idea
- it should be relevant to the topic
- it should create interest
- it should use language that everyone can understand
- it should require more than a guess to answer
- it should be used to emphasise key points
- it should relate to previous knowledge
- it should be a check of knowledge or understanding.

If you ask a question of the individual or the group, make sure that you know what the correct answer is.

When you get a response from a participant, it's a good idea to repeat the answer so that the rest of the group can hear the correct answer. Don't assume that because you heard the response everyone else did. Even if they did hear it, repetition provides overlearning.

When posing a question you must look around the group, not at anyone in particular. If you look at one person, it's an indication to everyone that the person you are looking at has been singled out to answer the question.

When you get an incorrect reply, don't damage the person's self-respect by saying 'No', 'Wrong', 'Stupid', or, my favourite, 'Once again for the dummies'. What you should do is acknowledge the reply and then prompt the person for the right answer by giving clues or suggestions. Alternatively, you can pass the question to the group for discussion.

All questions should be designed before the session and should be written on your session plan so that they are not overlooked or forgotten. This will also assist anyone else who uses your session notes.

Conclusion

Questions are an important part of the presenter's effectiveness. Without questions we would have little, if any, communication. Questions give the presenter feedback on both their own effectiveness and on the level of learning and understanding. They also give participants an indication of their relative performance.

When we design our session notes we should design the questions at the same time. They should be simple, straightforward questions, and not trick questions or questions to show how smart we are. Neither should they be used to fill in time.

We often use questions to find out if the participant or trainee can relate the new material to previously known materials. Never use questions as punishment.

When you get answers, make certain that you acknowledge the participant. If you neglect to do this, the participants may withdraw their attention.

Questions may be designed to involve the quiet ones in the group so have some easy questions planned. By getting these right, self-confidence is built and this leads to greater participation.

If a question is asked of you by a participant, try to get the group to answer it. This keeps them on their toes and thinking. If the group can't answer the question, try to reword it so that it can be answered by someone in the group. Give them clues or prompt them in the right direction. Make every effort to get the answer from the group. Rather than *tell* the individual or group, *ask* them.

Application example

As questioning style and techniques vary from presenter to presenter and trainer to trainer, it's difficult to give an example of how to design and use questions. It is important to remember that we are all different and that what works for one may not work for another. New presenters and trainers need to develop their own style of questioning.

Let's look at a training session on questioning. The trainer walks into the room, sits down and poses the question:

- 'What is a question?'

Before anyone in the group answers, the trainer starts the presentation. Posing this question has, the trainer hopes, started the group thinking.

As each important point in the presentation is reached, the trainer asks specific overhead–direct questions.

- 'What can we do if nobody in the group can answer our question?' (pause) 'Fred, can you tell us?'

At the end of the session the trainer generally asks a few preset questions that relate directly to the session objectives.

- 'What are ten points that we have to consider when we are designing a question?' 'One point each please. Wilma can you give me one?'

Of course, all of these questions were designed before the training took place. When they were designed they were included in the session plan so that they wouldn't be forgotten or overlooked.

Remember that at the end of a session we need to test to see if we have met our session objectives—by asking questions we can find out easily and quickly. Using questions is also a method of overlearning. The questions can usually be our conclusion, testing and summary all rolled into one if we have time constraints placed on us.

Further reading

Baird, L., Schneier, C. & Laird, D., *The Training and Development Sourcebook*, 2nd edn, Human Resource Press, Massachusetts, 1994.

Craig, Robert, *Training and Development Handbook*, 4th edn, McGraw-Hill Book Company, New York, 1996.

Honey, Peter, *The Trainer's Questionnaire Kit*, McGraw-Hill Book Company, New York, 1997.

Laird, Dugan, *Approaches to Training and Development*, 2nd edn, Addison-Wesley Publishing Company, Massachusetts, 1985.

Mager, Robert, *Measuring Instructional Results*, 2nd edn, Pitman Learning Company, California, 1984.

CHAPTER 12

Difficult situations and nerves

Now let's have a look at handling difficult situations and difficult participants. We will also look at a few methods that help to overcome that sweaty-palm syndrome. As well as tips for the new presenter and trainer, you will find included in this chapter some suggestions that may be relevant to experienced presenters and trainers who need to brush up a bit.

> You must learn to pause now and then
> so that things may catch up to you.

Dealing with difficult situations

All presenters get difficult participants or situations in their sessions. And it happens more often than we would like it to happen.

However difficult a situation seems to be, presenters need to keep their cool

What are some of the situations, and how can we handle them as professionals?

The group remains silent. It may help to ask the audience why they are bombarding you with their silence; it may be that they have a good reason. Perhaps you are covering material they have already been presented with. Perhaps they don't understand what's being presented, or perhaps your presentation method needs to be revised.

Things are moving too fast. Sometimes the group will become enthusiastic very quickly. This is good as long as you are prepared for it. You can ask for greater clarification of responses, ask for other participants to comment on responses or simply pose more difficult questions to the individuals or the group.

Things are moving too slowly. It's possible that the group isn't motivated to listen to your presentation. There are other reasons as well, but the same solutions apply. Ask for participant comments by nominating people to reply. Deliberately misstating information can spark comments from the group but if it doesn't, it's time to wake them up. You must give them a reason to listen and to become involved. Try to build on things they already know. Don't speed your presentation up to get them moving, it won't work.

A talkative participant. This is quite acceptable as long as the situation doesn't get out of hand. One or two talkative participants can add to the total value of the session. It's only if they become distracting to the rest of the group that you need to step in. Before you step in, try to use their peers to quieten them down. If that fails, you can cut the speaker off and summarise what he or she has said and then move straight on. If nothing else works, talk to them during a break, thank them for their input, but ask them to slow down a bit so that others may participate.

A silent participant. It may be that this person came along just to listen to the presentation. If you need them to participate, you might have to ask them some direct questions. Tread cautiously to start with by asking questions that can be answered fairly easily. If it happens to be a long-serving employee, it may be more relevant to ask them to share their experiences with the group.

The typical know-all. This person will know everything and they will correct, confront and contradict you. In most situations the group will sort this problem out for you. It's sometimes useful to get this person to take the notes. Another method is to put the know-all in your blind spot so that you may call on others more easily. This is called politely ignoring them. Don't get them offside, as their peers may feel for them.

Sessions getting sidetracked. Sometimes a discussion starts in the right direction but finishes up in the wrong place. The presenter must get it back on line. Perhaps ask the group if this is relevant to the topic or simply say that as interesting as it is, we only have enough time to cover the real issues. Make sure the group knows where they are heading to start with, then they can see when the discussion gets sidetracked.

Personality problems (between participants). Personality problems can distract everyone. If arguments start between participants, you must cut in quickly. Ask others for comments on the issue. Try to keep the personalities separated. If necessary, speak to them during a break and if the problem continues you may have to ask them (during a break) to keep their comments to themselves, or ask both of them to leave.

Personality problems (presenter and participant). Occasionally you will find that you have a personality clash with one of your participants. The professional public speaker must ignore this and continue treating the participant in a normal manner. Avoid letting the group see the problem.

The rambler. Some participants just ramble on, and on, and on. When they pause it's possible to ask them which point their comments are referring to, particularly if they have an outline of the session. You may have to politely cut them off by thanking them and moving straight on to the next issue. Interrupt politely and summarise before they finish, and cover all of the points you were after.

The arguer. The participant who argues might also have to be placed in a blind spot. Most of the time the group will ask the arguer to quieten down so the session can move on. Use your breaks again to talk to the person, telling them that others are being disadvantaged by their continuous objections. As a final step you may ask them to leave the group.

Complaints about other issues. Make sure that the participants know that the session will not be able to solve the world's problems. If you get complaints about the organisation, let them know that they can't change policy. If you spend time exploring such complaints, you'll be wasting the group's time on issues that can't be altered by them or you.

The side conversation. If you find that people become involved in side conversations, ask them to speak up so that the group can hear their comments on the issue. You'll find that this polite, non-threatening intervention will stop them from continuing. It may be that they can add some relevant information to the discussion.

The definitely wrong response. Don't embarrass any participant by telling them that they are wrong. What you can do is to acknowledge that they are entitled to their point of view and that is one way of looking at the situation. You can also summarise their response using the correct information. Another way is to ask the rest of the group for their comments on that particular response.

Planning the presentation

Planning and organisation are probably the most important points of your presentation. When they are under control everything may fall into place for you.

Planning includes all of your preparation, and organisation includes the information to be presented (this ties up with your objectives), who it's to be presented to, how it's to be presented and in what order.

It is rather like the planning and organisation of a three-course meal. The planning is the selection of the menu, deciding who to invite and the cooking of the meal. The presentation is the way the final meal looks and whether the guests want to eat it or not. This careful preparation assists in the avoidance of difficult situations and tends to settle the nerves as well. All that remains is to stop your hands from shaking as you serve the meal.

How to deal with anxiety

Anxiety or stress is a natural state that exists with presenters and trainers when they have to stand in front of a group. New presenters and trainers please take note—it doesn't disappear. What we manage to do with experience is to turn it to our advantage.

It is unlikely that there is a professional speaker or competent trainer who can stand in front of a group and still have a normal breathing rate, a dry shirt or blouse, a steady hand and a normal pulse rate every time they speak in front of a group.

Some of the problems new presenters and trainers face with their first public speaking experience are:

- the mouth going dry
- feeling like a stranger in 'strangerland'
- social barriers (age, sex, etc.)
- the subject matter.

Let's look at a number of methods in use that deal with the new presenter's nerves and butterflies. By following these tips you may be able to overcome your own nervousness.

One idea given to me many years ago was to imagine the audience sitting in front of me in the nude. That might be a bit of fun, but it can also be very distracting to your presentation. It may also increase your nervousness!

Here are some ideas that do work. Every person is different, so what works for one person, may not work for the next. As you read through these suggestions, put a mark beside the ones that you think might work for you.

- Be at ease and relax. Remember that the participants came to listen to you. They are not likely to begin by being negative.
- Breathe deeply as you walk down the corridor to the group. When people feel nervous their breathing is generally too shallow.
- As you walk down the corridor mentally rehearse the sequence of your presentation.
- Remember the self-fulfilling prophecy. If you think of yourself giving an excellent presentation you probably will. If you think of yourself making a fool of yourself, again you probably will.
- Again use the self-fulfilling prophecy and think of yourself as relaxed.
- Arrive early so you can settle in.
- Look professional. Dress the part and if you have course material with you make sure that they can see that you have done your prework. No need to hide it.
- Try to anticipate audience questions. Having anticipated the questions, work out the correct responses.
- Check all of your support equipment before the presentation so that you know everything is in working order.
- Create a physical setting that you feel comfortable with. If necessary it can be changed later.
- Use your session notes. You spent quite a bit of time preparing them, so use them effectively.
- Brainteasers make an interesting introduction if they can be made relevant to the presentation. They take the spotlight off you while you settle down.

- You need to be comfortable. Your notes should be in order and placed where you need them to be.
- If you're using a microphone, you must try it well in advance to get used to it. Make sure that it's properly adjusted for your use.
- Make sure that you establish your credibility during the beginning of the session.
- Using your session notes, give the group an outline of the presentation. Let them know what is to happen and what is expected.
- Motivate the group to listen to what you have to say. Give them a need to know.
- Practise your presentation beforehand. You may feel a little silly doing it to the bathroom mirror, but practice does make perfect. It's generally worthwhile to practise the beginning of your presentation a bit more than the rest. If you are serious about improvement you may even use a video or tape recorder. (Don't use the video in the bathroom as the lens tends to fog up.)
- Recognise that the tension you feel may be used effectively in your presentation. You may even plan this use in your notes, or try it in your practice session in the bathroom. Jump, throw your arms around, or maybe take the lead in a role-play.
- Move around. Don't stand fixed to one spot in front of the group. Walk around, but not so much that you then become a distraction.
- Warm up your voice before you start the presentation. Talk or sing to yourself. If that seems too silly, talk to the participants before the presentation starts.
- Keep eye contact with everyone in the group, and don't single out one or two people only.
- Pronounce your words clearly. Your audience needs to understand them all.
- Make sure that you know what you're talking about. If you don't, find out quickly or get someone else to do it. Presenters and trainers don't need to be experts in the subject matter, but they do have to have more than a good knowledge of the subject.
- If you have to sit in front of the group before your presentation, try some simple unobtrusive isometric exercises. Tense your muscles for a few seconds and then relax them, starting at the feet and working up to the head. Remember that these are unobtrusive exercises, so no-one will know that you are doing them.
- Attend appropriate courses in presentation techniques or public speaking.

- Remember that the average adult attention span is at most only around twenty minutes. Allow for breaks, they help you as well.
- Use the nine principles of learning, but in particular use group participation for nerve settling.
- Find out in advance who the participants are and what backgrounds they have.
- Admit your mistakes, but only if you make them. It may be of benefit to make the occasional mistake, this will let them see you as one of them. The mistake may also be used to check their understanding.
- You must always appear to be enthusiastic, even when you're not. With practice, anxiety can be changed to enthusiasm.
- Set up a video or tape recorder to see how you feel as a participant watching or listening to your session.
- Develop your own style of presentation. Don't always try to copy others.
- Get feedback from the participants. What you think you're saying may not be what they are hearing.
- Don't read from the text, the participants can read the material in their own time. This also allows you to use your own words, which are generally easier for the group to understand.
- Don't have heavy nights before a day of presentations. You need to be well rested and on your toes.

Conclusion

Feeling dry in the mouth and having a few nervous twitches are normal for all public speakers, presenters and trainers, both new and experienced. If you don't feel at least a little bit anxious it may be time to look for a new challenge in your career.

Put your mind into gear before opening your mouth. This is good advice for anyone but is particularly important for someone standing in front of a group.

It's important for public speakers to be polite to everyone in the group. If we aren't we may find that the group turns on us if we pick on someone, even if that person is someone the whole group appears not to tolerate.

If you have a difficult participant, try to use the peer pressure in the group to sort the problem out for you. Peer pressure is an excellent way of overcoming such problems, so use it to your advantage.

Don't single people out in a group situation; instead, talk to them during breaks. You may have to call extra breaks occasionally.

A number of methods useful for calming nerves have been included in this chapter. Use them, all of them, if possible. Not only will it be easier for you to present your session, it will make it easier for your participants to absorb the information.

Application example

Before becoming a public speaker you probably attended a number of presentations given by other people. It is likely that you witnessed a number of difficult situations. Think back on those presentations and see if you can recall how they were handled by the presenter. The next time you sit in the audience of a presentation, watch specifically for these situations and see if the methods used will suit your style.

Further reading

Donaldson, Les & Scannell, Edward, *Human Resource Development: The New Trainer's Guide*, 2nd edn, Addison-Wesley Publishing Company, Massachusetts, 1986, Chapters 16 & 18.

Hughes, Shirley, *Professional Presentations*, McGraw-Hill Book Company, Sydney, 1990.

Kalish, Karen, *How To Give A Terrific Presentation*, Amacom, New York, 1997.

CHAPTER 13

Motivation and attention

Why do you continue to do certain things and not others? Why do you listen only to some people?

It's all to do with motivation and the way our attention is held. If we want our participants to learn, we must motivate them to listen to us and ensure that we keep their attention. When we make a presentation, who do you think is responsible for the individual's learning? The presenter is.

What is motivation?

Motivation is the urge in the individual to have a need filled. The need or urge becomes more powerful when it's not being satisfied.

The more motivated the participants are, the easier it is for the presenter to present his or her information effectively. If the participants are not motivated to listen or learn, they are almost certainly wasting their time and yours.

Believe it or not, the presenter is responsible in most cases for motivating the participants. It doesn't happen automatically. But before we look at some motivation techniques, we need to recognise that there are two types of motivation. The first type is where participants know that they must perform in the course or they may suffer severe consequences. This is referred to as a negative motivator. The second and more effective form of motivation is when the participants simply want to learn. This form of motivation creates a more pleasant learning atmosphere. Knowing the difference between these is more important for the trainer rather than the public speaker.

We will be dealing only with the second form of motivation as it's the one normally used. The threatening form of motivation is used in extreme situations where other methods may not work or have already failed.

How do we motivate a participant?

If we believe that motivation is the urge in the individual to have a need filled, wouldn't it be logical to say that if we could identify what need the participants have, we could motivate or interest them to listen? This is almost right, but it needs some refining.

If we've done our job properly the group will respond to the information that the course or presentation is based on. This information should tie in with their needs, which should have been correctly identified in the needs analysis.

At the beginning of the first few sessions the presenter can allow the group to contribute ideas about the direction of the course and the selection of specific topic areas. This type of course is commonly referred to as user-driven. If the group has this input, it then becomes its own design. With this design comes a sense of ownership, which is a great motivator. If the group thinks that it has chosen the topic areas, it can't complain during the course that you have given irrelevant information.

You will probably find that the areas identified by the group in this situation match up with your course objectives. If they do not match up exactly you may have to provide a bit of subtle direction.

You have to let the individuals know that by listening or participating in your session they will have some of their needs filled. It's up to you to identify these needs and describe them. These needs can come from many different areas: social needs, safety needs, security needs, status, new technology, promotion opportunities, new machinery, new methods, or simply an easier way to do the job.

If the individuals realise that their needs will be met, they are usually eager to learn

Motivating the participants is similar to dangling the proverbial carrot in front of them, but they always get the carrot when they finish.

Regardless of what your session is about, you can always find some reason for encouraging the participants to listen. Once the reason has been stated it creates the motivation.

There are a number of motivation theories and they are interesting to read and study. However, the easiest and most practical thing new presenters can do is to ask themselves 'If I were a participant in this program, why should I listen to me?'.

If you pose this question you will always find some motivating response, even if it takes several minutes. But don't stop at one. The more reasons you can give for people to listen to your presentation the more they will be motivated. Remember too, it's the presenter's responsibility to remind the participants that they want to learn and to supply them with the incentive.

> People do things for their reasons,
> not yours
> or the organisation's.

You may need to recapture the participants' attention during a session, so keep some tactics in reserve

It may also help if you keep one or two of the motivators up your sleeve in case things start to drag and you need to fire their motivation or grab attention again during the session.

Even if you're involved in a presentation that hasn't been designed for a stated need through a presentation or training needs analysis, you can talk to the group before the session starts to identify its needs. If this can't be done, you should plan a few minutes at the beginning of the session to find the needs and link the session to those needs.

If you think it sounds as though you're becoming a salesperson, you're right. You must sell your reasons for motivation to all of the individuals in the group.

Using the nine principles of learning properly will help to create motivation and will also allow you to keep the group's interest during the session. Make sure that you use them effectively.

Conclusion

It's important that we motivate the individuals in the group to want to listen, learn or participate. Without motivation they won't do anything. Once we have created motivation we sometimes still need to remind the group of its reasons for wanting to learn. By using these reminders, and the nine principles of adult learning, we can keep the group's attention.

We must know our audience in advance so that we can identify its motivators. Sometimes we only find out about our audience thirty minutes before the session commences. A good presenter is flexible and will adapt to suit the specific group needs as they appear.

Application example

The day is hot, the winds are calm and it feels like a holiday atmosphere. Can you imagine sitting in an open theatre or classroom next to a white sandy beach, overlooking the warm waters on a tropical island? That's what your participants see, but you've been given a four-hour session to present on law. Some solutions have to be found for this interesting problem.

For this presentation the speaker had to find out very quickly (only a couple of days before the session started) what the needs of the group were. The presenter found that the participants were very concerned about implications of both omission and commission. This piece of information was what the presenter needed for the group's motivation and attention.

The session started with the presenter nominating participants to act in various roles—judge, jury, defendant, recorders and other court personnel.

Before any questions were asked the presenter explained that one of the participants had been charged in the areas of omission and commission during the supervision of the plaintiff's daughter. Their task was to listen to the evidence and pass judgment (and possibly sentence) on the defendant.

Sometimes a dramatic illustration can be invaluable in getting the group's attention

Everybody was motivated to listen and participate as the presenter had found an excellent reason for them to listen. This need was found by simply talking to them.

The next thing to happen after the ground rules had been set was for a number of pallbearers to carry in a coffin containing, supposedly, the blood-covered body of the plaintiff's daughter. The coffin was placed in the centre of the 'classroom'.

Do you think the presenter had the group's attention? It could have been snowing green snow and the group wouldn't have noticed!

Further reading

Baird, L., Schneier, C. & Laird, D., *The Training and Development Sourcebook*, 2nd edn, Human Resource Press, Massachusetts, 1994.

Donaldson, Les & Scannell, Edward, *Human Resource Development: The New Trainer's Guide*, 2nd edn, Addison-Wesley Publishing Company, Massachusetts, 1986, Chapter II.

Heerman, Barry, *Building Team Spirit*, McGraw-Hill Book Company, New York, 1997.

Kalish, Karen, *How To Give A Terrific Presentation*, Amacom, New York, 1997.

Owens, Robert, *Organisational Behaviour in Education*, 5th edn, Prentice-Hall International, New Jersey, 1994.

CHAPTER 14

Barriers to effective communication

All speakers must recognise that there are many barriers to effective communication with both individuals and with a group of people.

In this chapter I will attempt to give you most of the common barriers to effective communication so that you may be able to recognise them should you experience any of them. Not only should you recognise them, you must fix them.

What is effective communication?

Before starting it will help if we define what communication is. Unfortunately, there are still some people who think communication is simply being able to give clear directions or information. This understanding of communication is only half right.

Communication is the effective giving and receiving of information. To be effective, the message must be understood by both the communicator and the receiver. If the message isn't clearly or easily understood, there is a problem that needs to be rectified. Such problems are our barriers to effective communication.

In most communication models we have a message (the instruction) that needs to be given to another person. When the message sender (the speaker) selects who to give the message to (the participant) he or she needs to select an appropriate medium for the sending of the message. The message is then sent in the appropriate form and received. The message receiver interprets the message and perhaps adds his or her own meaning to some or all of it. As this is a fairly complicated exercise, there is always the chance of things going wrong.

The only way to find out if the message has been received and understood without any distortion is to get feedback from the message receiver.

This process of message sending and receiving may use the spoken word, non-verbal gestures, written information or any other means that you can think of.

You must realise that, regardless of which process you're using, all are susceptible to distortion or misunderstanding.

Communication does not occur unless there is a clear understanding by both parties

What are the common barriers?

The use of long words by the speaker is quite often a problem. Have you been in a presentation where the speaker has tried to impress the participants with long words? You normally find that nobody is prepared to ask what they all mean as they have a fear of looking ignorant in front of the group. Use only easily understood language.

Using new words is quite valid as long as you realise that they are new to the group and that you explain their meaning.

Jargon should be avoided unless it's relevant to the presentation or to the group's general knowledge. If it is used, its meaning must be explained. Jargon can be difficult to identify as we often use it without even noticing. We also have the situation where your participants might not ask what it means for fear of looking ignorant.

Language differences are becoming more of a problem as we have an increasing percentage of different language groups at our venues. Make sure that you speak clearly and keep testing for message understanding.

Feedback helps us to find out if our message has been properly understood

When the non-verbal message does not match the verbal message there is a barrier. We can't afford to create confusion by having our non-verbal communication saying something different to our verbal communication.

If presentation aids don't match the topic we again create confusion. When we select our presentation aids we must make certain that they are appropriate to the topic.

If the presentation aids don't work when they're supposed to the participants may lose interest. Check before starting that all of your presentation aids work, particularly models and samples you have ready for the group to use.

A boring presentation can be one of your biggest barriers to effective communication. If you are presenting a boring topic, you must find a way to liven it up. If you're simply a boring presenter, design the session in such a way that your own presentation interests the group. Focus on the participants' needs.

Assuming they know all of the things that should be prerequisite to them attending your presentation is a barrier. You need to check existing levels of knowledge at the very beginning of your presentation. Make sure that your session builds on existing participant knowledge.

The way we say things can affect the meaning and therefore the understanding. Most speakers and trainers, without realising it, tend to speak louder when they're talking about important sections of their presentation. Try to change this around, so the participants might pay more attention to the minor points of the presentation. Think about your projection and inflections.

Participant and speaker preconceptions have to match up. Any preconceived ideas the participants have about the presentation must be accurate. Make certain that the participants know what the presentation is about before it starts. It's also a good idea to send out course information to the participants well before the course commences.

By listening to the individuals and the group you'll find out if your message is getting through clearly and safely. Remember that communication is a two-way process and that you have to get feedback from the group continually to check understanding.

Make sure that the trainees know in advance what the training session will be about

| Why do some participants not listen?

In addition to the previous list of barriers, we also need to recognise some other reasons why the participants may not be listening to your presentation. If your participants are not listening, you could safely say that communication has broken down.

You must realise that people think faster than your speaking rate, so pace your presentation to stop their minds from wandering. Most presenters and trainers find it best if the pace varies during the session.

Effective listening requires you to give the group members some motivation. If they do not know why they should listen to your presentation, they probably will not listen.

Distractions also interfere with listening. When the participants are distracted by your upside-down overhead transparency, or by the handout that you've given out too early, they concentrate on the distraction and not your presentation.

If the information becomes too complicated, effective listening stops. If you have complicated information to pass on, make a point of breaking the information down into small, easily understandable pieces. Check the group's understanding before moving on to the next piece and so avoid information overload.

> ONE SHOULD NOT AIM AT BEING
> POSSIBLE TO UNDERSTAND,
> ONE SHOULD AIM AT BEING
> IMPOSSIBLE TO MISUNDERSTAND.

Poor communication may result in:
- poor training of staff
- misunderstandings
- conflict between staff
- objectives not being met
- frustration
- organisational inefficiency.

Alternatively, if the information is too simple, your participants will again let their thoughts drift elsewhere. Once the mind starts wandering, effective listening stops. Your presentation must be challenging to the individuals.

Many books and articles have been written on effective listening skills. I suggest that you find an article or two and read them. It's imperative that the speaker is a good listener as well as a good presenter.

Conclusion

We want the participants to interpret the information correctly. To receive the message without distortion the individuals must be listening attentively. It also helps if the group respects you as a presenter or trainer. You need to gain this respect, it doesn't just come with the job.

Ask yourself whether this is the best way to get your message across. It may be that there are more effective ways. Whichever is the easiest way for the participants to understand is the one that should be used. Make certain that you always consider the receiver.

Even simple communication needs to be planned in advance. If you don't understand your message, how is someone else supposed to understand you?

Communication is the effective process of information giving and receiving, but to be effective the message must be understood by both the communicator and the receiver. Always follow up your message.

Application example

As a new presenter it's sometimes interesting to talk with your group informally after the presentation. You may find that things you thought were perfectly clear have been interpreted in a completely different way.

Make mental notes of the reasons for the misunderstanding. Don't try to defend your communication; if the correct message didn't get across, you need to modify the delivery.

When working with other speakers or trainers, it's a good idea to offer constructive criticism on the communication. It's sometimes very difficult to identify the barriers by yourself, so help each other improve effective communication skills. But ensure that it's constructive criticism and not destructive criticism!

Further reading

Bishop, Sue, *Training Games for Assertiveness and Conflict Resolution*, McGraw-Hill Book Company, New York, 1997.

Craig, Robert, *Training and Development Handbook*, 4th edn, McGraw-Hill Book Company, New York, 1996.

Donaldson, Les & Scannell, Edward, *Human Resource Development: The New Trainer's Guide*, 2nd edn, Addison-Wesley Publishing Company, Massachusetts, 1986, Chapter 9.

Heerman, Barry, *Building Team Spirit*, McGraw-Hill Book Company, New York, 1997.

Kalish, Karen, *How To Give A Terrific Presentation*, Amacom, New York, 1997.

CHAPTER 15

Non-verbal communication

If you want your participants to be enthusiastic about your presentation you need to communicate your enthusiasm to them. A speaker standing nervously in front of a group and holding on to the lectern for dear life isn't going to project enthusiasm. Even before the presenter has said anything the group knows what to expect. On the other hand, a speaker who is dressed appropriately and looks relaxed and enthusiastic will have much more chance of reaching the session objectives.

Recent studies indicate that around 65 per cent of our communication is done through non-verbal signals. Speakers should be experts in communication, so it follows that they must know about these signals. Non-verbal communication is also referred to as body language, which is a study by itself. However, to assist the new presenter we will attempt to identify a number of the most common non-verbal communications the presenter is likely to encounter.

What is non-verbal communication?

Non-verbal communication is anything that can alter or reinforce the message in any form of communication. If you think that this is a very broad definition and covers all types of communication, you are right.

Your facial expression is just part of your non-verbal communication

We communicate non-verbally by the way we dress, our posture, the expressions on our face, the amount of eye contact used, the way we position our hands, the way we touch things and the way we listen.

Even a simple statement can have its meaning altered or reinforced by the way we shrug our shoulders when we put it to the group, by the use of inflection when we say it, by the way it is written or typed when we give it out as a handout. Perhaps the figure of 65 per cent is extremely conservative.

Gestures, dress and posture all add meaning to what we actually say

What gestures should we be aware of?

Some participants require more personal space than others. If they don't have this space, they feel uncomfortable and therefore do not pay attention to the presentation. Watch for signs.

If you ask a participant whether he or she understands what you're talking about and the answer is 'yes', make sure that the head gesture (nodding) matches, and isn't in conflict with the stated response.

When a question is being asked of you, you should watch the person asking it. It is sometimes easy to pick up clues as to what he or she really wants to know.

If participants cover their mouths while you are speaking, it may indicate that they don't believe you. It may be worthwhile checking this before you go further.

If your participants use both their hands to support their heads, it's time to change your tactics as boredom has set in.

When the head is supported by one hand and that hand has a finger pointing vertically, it suggests that the person is evaluating the information you've just given.

If people in the group start pulling at their collars, it may indicate that they are getting angry and need to let off some steam.

Should your participants start rubbing their hands together, watch out—you may be being conned.

Palm gestures are not often used in lecture theatres or training rooms as the participants are usually seated. However, if someone presents you with open palms, it's safe to assume that he or she is being totally honest with you.

A church steeple formed by the hands is used by people who know everything about the subject. Find out if they do have the knowledge. If they have, encourage them to participate and offer their ideas. Look for their support.

Similarly the person who thinks they know everything may adopt a sitting back position with the hands clasped behind the head. Check his or her understanding and knowledge and try to enlist their support.

Folded arms can indicate that the participant has put up a barrier. However, when people sit for long periods of time they tend to fold their arms more often.

How can we detect uncertainty?

If we ask participants a question and, while they are responding, they attempt to cover their mouths, it may indicate that they are trying to hide what they are saying.

Similarly, if people rub their noses while answering or talking, it may again indicate that they are uncertain or lying about their response.

Looking down and rubbing an eye can also indicate a lie or uncertainty. It may indicate that they can't see, or don't want to see, the point you are making.

These points are only indicators and should not be taken as gospel. These gestures merely give you an indication that a person may not be telling the truth, or does not believe what you are saying.

Are all people the same?

Each sex, social class, age, nationality, race or culture has its own set of built-in non-verbal signals. When a person is educated in a society, not only is he or she taught the words or spoken language, but also the non-verbal signals of that society.

For this reason we can't say that because a person uses a specific gesture, he or she is communicating a known message. For example, in some societies, if eye contact is avoided it can indicate that a person may be hiding the truth when asked a question. In other societies, this same gesture may indicate respect for the person asking the question.

We need to be aware of our own preconceived ideas. You may think it's easy to classify some participants on one or two non-verbal actions, but question yourself on the interpretation you've made. Non-verbal signals sometimes need to be clarified as do verbal signals when we are uncertain of the meaning.

Conclusion

It's easy to see that we do rely heavily on the non-verbal gestures given by others. If we ignore them, we may not get the whole picture. If we do take them in, it may lead us to what the participant really is thinking. At the very least, it reinforces what they are saying.

One signal or gesture by itself probably won't indicate anything at all. What we should be doing is looking for groups of signals. If we notice two gestures that have similar interpretations, we should take action on them, at least by checking the participant's message.

Not only do these gestures apply to the participants, but they also apply to you as the presenter. When you say something to the group you have to ensure that your non-verbal signals match your message. Don't say yes to someone in the group while shaking your head from side to side, or when you tell the group that you are open to questions make sure that your arms aren't folded tightly across your chest.

Remember that non-verbal communication is important to both the delivering and receiving of a message. Don't try to hide your own non-verbal signals.

Application example

Most of the time we are unaware of our own non-verbal signals. In Chapter 14 I suggested that if you use another speaker to check your effective communication with a group, he or she would be able to offer constructive criticism. This would also apply to your non-verbal communication with the group.

If this is impractical or impossible, why not set up a video camera in the back of your classroom? Then you will be able to see all of the things you wouldn't have believed you were doing.

Once you start to understand non-verbal signals, you will find that not only do you look for them in a presentation or training situation, you will look for them outside the venue or classroom as well. It may even become part of your normal communication process.

Further reading

Bishop, Sue, *Training Games for Assertiveness and Conflict Resolution*, McGraw-Hill Book Company, New York, 1997.

Kalish, Karen, *How To Give A Terrific Presentation*, Amacom, New York, 1997.

Pease, Allan, *Body Language*, Camel Publishing Company, Sydney, 1981.

CHAPTER 16

Presentation aids

We learn   1% through taste
               1.5% through touch
               3.5% through smell
               11% through hearing
               83% through sight
We remember 10% of what we read
               20% of what we hear
               30% of what we see
               50% of what we see and hear
               80% of what we say
               90% of what we say and do

What are presentation aids?

Presentation aids are, strictly, aids to your presentation or to the learning process. They are not a crutch for the presenter or instructor to lean on, or something that we feel we must use all the time.

Presentation aids are something that the presenter or trainer can use, with or without words, which facilitate the students' learning. Visual aids are things that the participants can see. Research has indicated that the average participant will remember only about 20 per cent of what they hear and that they remember between 50 per cent and 80 per cent of what they both hear and see. When we listen, our mind appears to be very selective about what it remembers. It seems to pick up only the things that it's interested in and ignores the rest of the information.

However, if we combine some form of visual aid with the talking, it seems to reinforce key words in the mind. We must take advantage of these aids as this can increase the participants' power of recall by 250 per cent to 400 per cent.

If the presentation aids are used in a simple and logical manner, it not only makes the session easier for the participant but also for the presenter. Another thing that makes it easier for the speaker is that it ensures some consistency in repeat presentations. Presentation aids also allow other presenters to assist as they too can 'read' what has to be covered. (Obviously they would combine the session notes with the presentation aids to get the whole picture.)

Presentation aids can also create interest in the subject. If the aids are presented properly they should catch the participants' attention and get them into a learning frame of mind. What we do need to be aware of though is not to become a facilitator of presentation aids. If people only come along to watch the show they probably won't be learning anything. Be wise and be selective.

When you use presentation aids, make sure that all of the participants can see, hear, touch, smell or taste whatever it is you want them to.

Most professional speakers or trainers use a variety of presentation aids or training aids to keep the audience interested.

Not all presentation aids need to be expensive. As most presentation aids are visual aids, they need to be tidy in appearance and generally attractive. They need to be able to hold the audience's attention and get key points across.

The purpose of visual aids

- They arouse and maintain interest.
- They simplify instruction.
- They accelerate learning as more senses are involved.
- They aid retention if a strong impact is created.

Types of presentation aids

Overhead projector

The **overhead projector** is now one of the more commonly used presentation aids. It is an electronically operated machine with a light source at the base which is reflected up to the projection head. From the projection head the light is projected to a screen or wall. Between the light source at the base and the projection head we place a transparency (a clear film) containing the information we want the audience to see. Look at the diagram on page 116.

When using an overhead projector for the first time, make sure that you're comfortable with it. This means that you should be in an empty room practising with one and becoming proficient.

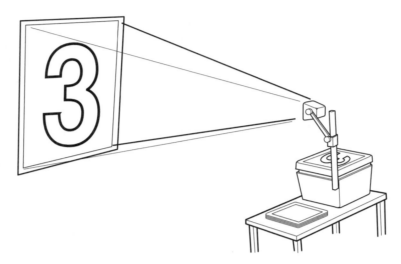

The overhead projector is a very useful training aid

When using an overhead projector, all presenters should check whether:
- the room is too light
- the projector is in focus
- the transparency is the right way round
- the lettering is large enough
- everyone can see the screen
- you need a pointer
- you have a sheet of paper for revealing bits at a time
- a spare globe is available.

If you move the overhead projector during your presentation you will need to refocus it if you place it in a slightly different position.

Chapter 17 gives much more information on the overhead projector and the production of transparencies.

Videos

Video systems are relatively new in the area of public speaking and training. They are generally more appropriate for training situations than public speaking. When we refer to 'video' we are not talking only about video tapes, but we are also referring to the use of video cameras for presentation and training purposes.

Currently, four types of video are available:
- U matic (20 mm wide tape)
- VHS (12 mm wide tape)
- Beta (12 mm wide tape)
- Video 8 (8 mm wide tape).

A video camera can be used for on-the-spot filming in the classroom and prerecorded tapes can be most instructive too

Most of the videos we purchase for training are the same as the 16 millimetre or 35 millimetre films we purchase or hire. The advantage of having them on video tape though is that we have a much smaller package to carry around and, more importantly, we can usually use them in a lighted situation. This allows the participants to make notes if they wish to.

Using the video camera is possibly one of the most enlightening experiences your participants can have. When you tell individuals that they fiddle with their pens too much when they are counselling someone and they don't really believe you, all you now have to do is replay the tape and let them see for themselves.

When using the video camera and player there are a number of things to consider. Listed below are the ones that the new presenter must be aware of:

- Preview recorded tapes before the session.
- Use only one prerecorded tape for the session.
- Ensure you have enough power outlets.
- Make sure all the participants can see the screen.
- Make sure there is a minimum of reflection on the screen during playback.
- Rewind all tapes when finished.
- Turn the monitor off when not in use.
- Keep the lens cap on the camera when not in use.
- Don't zoom or pan too much with the camera.
- Try to capture non-verbal signs of the role-players.
- Allow time for the tapes to be reviewed by the group.
- Be thoroughly familiar with the equipment.
- Try to have spares standing by (just in case).

If you intend using a 16 mm film projector be sure that you are practised in its operation

Films

Films used to be very popular with trainers. As the result of problems associated with carrying large film containers from class to class and carrying heavy projectors around, we now see them being replaced with videos.

The 16 millimetre film can be an extremely effective training aid. Normally, these films are narrated by a well-known personality or an expert in the field and have a lot of impact.

Projectors for 16 millimetre film aren't easy to set up and the presenter or an assistant must enter the training room well before the session to prepare for the screening.

To use a film projector effectively, make sure you read the instruction booklet or get someone to show you how to use it. If you get someone to show you, these are the things that you should be asking:

- Where should I set it up?
- How do I load it?
- How do I rewind the film?
- How does it pack up?
- Where is the spare globe?
- When can I preview the film?
- Can I try it now?

Whiteboards

As new training rooms are being built the chalkboard is gradually being replaced with **whiteboards**. In fact, it is rare that any venue has a

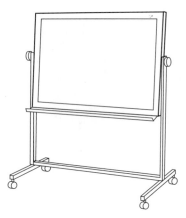

The mobile whiteboard can double as an overhead projector screen

chalkboard. A whiteboard is a smooth white-surfaced board which can be written on with special whiteboard markers. The white surface is much nicer to look at in contrast to the darker coloured chalkboards.

Whiteboards are generally mounted on portable wheeled frames, which allows us to have a portable training room. This portability makes it an attractive proposition for the management of most organisations. They can also be mounted on walls as a permanent fixture or set up on a portable frame.

As with the use of most presentation aids, there are a number of things to remember when using the whiteboard:

- Have the whiteboard positioned so that everyone can see it.
- Write large enough for everyone to see it.
- Write legibly (if you can't, practise).
- Put the cap on the marker when you're not using it (they dry out very quickly).
- Use a variety of colours.
- Use the eraser provided to erase with.
- Plan your board layout before you start writing.
- Don't put too much on the board.
- Never talk to the board. Write, then turn and talk.
- Practise drawing straight lines, circles and letters on the whiteboard as often as possible.
- If you use the whiteboard as a projection screen, make sure that the reflection off the screen is not directed at anyone in the group. (Check the back of the screen, it may have a matt projection finish.)
- Don't bang the tip of the whiteboard marker on the board, it pushes the tip back into the casing and makes it useless.

Chalkboards are still popular and can be used very effectively

Chalkboards

Chalkboards are not a very common sight in training rooms any more. The principle here is to have a matt-painted surface which can be written on using a piece of chalk. Gone are the days of having chalk dust everywhere, as we can now purchase dustless and squeakless chalk.

There are a few tricks you can use with a chalkboard. Some of them are detailed below:

- Plan your layout before you start writing.
- Don't put too much on the board at once.
- Always erase with the duster provided.
- Use coloured chalk to highlight.
- Make fast, firm strokes with the chalk.
- Never talk to the board. Write, then turn and talk.
- Hold the chalk between your thumb and the first two fingers with about 1–2 centimetres of chalk projecting.
- Rotate the chalk as you write to keep a good writing point.
- Use templates to assist with the drawing of diagrams.
- Using a diagram on a large sheet of paper, go along the lines punching pin holes. Hold the paper up on the board and tap it with the duster. When you take the paper away simply join the dots for a professional diagram. All this is done before the group comes in.
- Use an overhead projector to project your diagrams up on the chalkboard. Then copy them before the group comes in.
- Practise drawing straight lines, circles and letters on the chalkboard as often as possible.

Feltboards

Feltboards or blanket boards may be used for the display of any prepared materials. If you have a series of diagrams that you wish to use, stick some coarse sandpaper on the back of them. The sandpaper will attach to the felt surface.

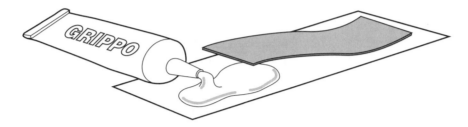

If you prepare training materials well in advance, the feltboard is an ideal way to display them

Magnetic boards

Magnetic boards are usually a painted sheet of steel. The boards themselves are not magnetic but the things we stick on them are. Again, if you have a series of diagrams that you wish to present, it's a matter of sticking magnets on the back of your diagrams. Magnets like the ones we use to hold notes on refrigerator doors are ideal and can now be purchased quite easily. Sometimes you may find that your whiteboard is also a magnetic board.

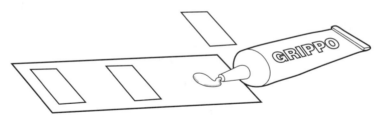

Try using a magnetic board to set up posters or other training material

Charts and posters

Prepared **flip charts** or **posters** can be used effectively. With prepared flip charts you may have a lot of standard information that would take too long to write up on a board. With posters you may find that there is something printed that directly relates to the specified subject. When you are finished using these items, remove them before they become a distraction to the group.

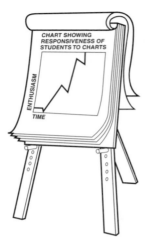

Flip charts can be prepared long before the training session

Handouts

Handouts are an ideal presentation aid if we use them correctly. Don't give your handouts to the participants at the beginning of the session unless you want them to read the notes right away. If you want the participants to work through the notes with you, tell them as you give them out. It's common for the handouts to be given at the end of the session.

If the handout covers most of your presentation, tell the participants at the beginning of the session. This practice will allow the participants to give you their undivided attention, as they will not have to make their own notes.

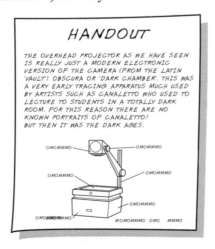

Printed handouts can save the trainees a lot of time

Tape recorders

Even the most basic equipment can be effective as a training aid if it is used imaginatively

Tape recorders are not commonly used in presentations because most speakers say that a participant will not sit and listen to a tape recording, but it is up to the presenter to use this presentation aid effectively. It doesn't always have to be a tape of someone speaking. What about using it for sound effects, or playing music? If we're to give a presentation on Tchaikovsky, wouldn't a prerecorded tape of Tchaikovsky's Symphony No. 6 in B minor be applicable? (Perhaps it could be used as an introduction.)

Slides

A **slide** presentation can be used as an excellent break from the routine. Slides are easy to plan and keep up to date but as you do need a darkened room with a slide show, keep it brief. It's also possible to use a slide/tape presentation. A recorded sound tape is used and is synchronised with a series of slides. This allows the presenter to plug in, push the button and enjoy the presentation or pass additional comments over the top of the narrator. The slide/tape presentation does require special equipment to prepare and to playback.

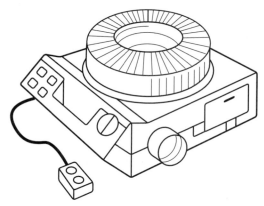

Slide presentations can be kept up to date easily, or varied for different groups

---

Essentials for good visual aids

- They need to be simple and easy to understand.
- They need to be brief and concise.
- They need to stress essential points.
- They need to be the correct size and clearly visible.
- They need to be interesting.
- They should have the right colours, spacing, etc.
- They must be applicable to the subject.

Advantages and disadvantages

Let's look briefly at some of the advantages and disadvantages of the presentation aids discussed.

Overhead projector

Advantages: Lets the speaker face the group at all times
                     Instant placement or removal of information
                     May be used in normal lighting conditions

Disadvantages: Costly to purchase
                     Bulky to transport between locations
                     Requires extra preparation

Films

Advantages: Most are professionally produced
                     Visually dynamic and portray action
                     Overcomes the problem of inaccessible places

Disadvantages: Tend to be quickly outdated
                     Expensive to purchase
                     Need to be used in dim light

Videos

Advantages: Most are professionally produced
                     Can be used under normal lighting conditions
                     Generally can be hired on a short term

Disadvantages: Can be expensive to purchase
                     Requires special equipment for use
                     Different types of format

Chalkboards
Advantages:

Inexpensive to purchase

Consumables easy to obtain

Can use a variety of colours

Disadvantages:

Tends to get messy on hands and clothes

Not common in different locations

May require a lot of prework

Whiteboards
Advantages:

Generally portable

Consumables easy to obtain

Can use a variety of colours

Disadvantages:

Expensive to purchase

Pens dry out quickly

Slippery to write on (unless practised)

Feltboards
Advantages:

Inexpensive to make

Easy to make portable

Can use existing artwork and can be reused

Disadvantages:

Not common

Wind can blow artwork off board

Some people think they are for children

Magnetic boards
Advantages:

Relatively inexpensive

Able to use existing artwork and can be reused

Can improvise if needed (use a filing cabinet)

Disadvantages:

Not common

Magnets lose their magnetism

Some people think they are for children

Charts and posters
Advantages:

Improved colour and quality

Easy to carry around

Allows material to be prepared and reused

Disadvantages:

Tend to damage easily

May become a distraction if not moved

May require a lot of prework

Handouts

Advantages: Inexpensive to produce

Can provide background material not covered

A permanent reference to trainees

Disadvantages: May require a lot of prework

Can be a distraction if not timed properly

May contradict what the speaker is saying

Tape recorders

Advantages: Tapes inexpensive to purchase

Very portable

Adds variety to the presentation

Disadvantages: May require a lot of prework

Cannot be used too often

Player system may be expensive

Slides

Advantages: Simple to use and high entertainment value

Presenter able to set the pace

Easy to edit to bring up to date or alter

Disadvantages: Time consuming to produce

Requires darkened room

Cannot show motion

Conclusion

Not only do presentation aids make the learning process easier, but they make it more enjoyable. Don't be afraid of applying creativity to your presentation. Also don't be afraid to adopt someone else's ideas either—it is a compliment after all.

We can see that there are a great number of presentation aids available and a good presenter has a working knowledge of all of them. Use as many of them as possible so that you're familiar with all of them. You never know when you may have to fill in for someone else who uses different types of aids.

Presentation aids improve learning significantly if they're used with imagination and contain relevant information.

Presentation aids assist us in communicating our knowledge and ideas to the audience. We should continually be looking at ways to improve or update our presentation aids. We could also think about combining some of our aids if necessary.

The presenter who is always looking for new ways to communicate probably uses presentation aids creatively

All of our presentation aids must be presented with a sense of purpose. The participant must be able to see the purpose and relevance.

Possibly one of the best presentation aids we have is the individual participant. We haven't discussed the possibility of using our audience members as a presentation aid. How do you think you could use them effectively?

Further reading

Craig, Robert, *Training and Development Handbook*, 4th edn, McGraw-Hill Book Company, New York, 1996.

Hughes, Shirley, *Professional Presentations*, McGraw-Hill Book Company, Sydney, 1990.

Kalish, Karen, *How To Give A Terrific Presentation*, Amacom, New York, 1997.

Laird, Dugan, *Approaches to Training and Development*, 2nd edn, Addison-Wesley Publishing Company, Massachusetts, 1985.

CHAPTER 17

Using an overhead projector

The overhead projector is now one of the most popular forms of presentation aids in use today and for this reason we will devote a whole chapter to it.

Overhead projectors are now found in most training rooms and conference venues. If the facility cannot supply an overhead projector we can always take one with us from our base. This means too, that we don't have to rely on proper training or conference rooms. All we have to do is find a location with a power outlet and a light coloured wall to project onto. This isn't an ideal situation, but it would probably be better than nothing.

Most presenters and trainers have their own prepared overhead transparencies for any type of presentation they need to give. Presenters find them ideal in most cases as they are compact and durable. A lot of prepared training packages that we can now purchase have overhead transparencies supplied with them, as well as a session plan stating when they should be used.

By using prepared overhead transparencies we can both strengthen and shorten our presentation.

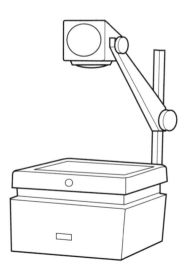

Transparencies for the overhead projector can be prepared well in advance of the session

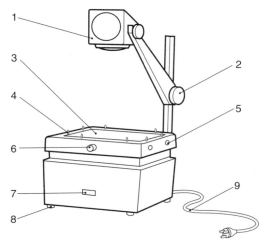

1. Projection head/lens
2. Focusing knob
3. Fresnel lens/top plate
4. Locating pins for cardboard frames
5. Screws for roll feed attachments
6. Top plate catch
7. On/off switch
8. Levelling legs
9. Power cord

The competent presenter knows how all the presentation aids function

The parts of an overhead projector

Presenters should make sure that they understand the functions of the different parts of an overhead projector (see the diagram above).

There are now different types of overhead projectors around. Some are fixed units, some are fold-up units and some have built-in spares. However, you will find that they are all similar in their basic design. Check which type you have or will be using.

Where do we use it?

It's normal to have the overhead projector set up in front of the room. When positioning the equipment, ensure that everyone in the audience will be able to see the screen. If you have an adjustable stand to place the overhead projector on, you may adjust it right down so that someone seated can see over the top of it.

Ideally, the stand used for the overhead projector will have enough room on the side to hold your session notes and prepared transparencies.

The projection should be aimed reasonably high on the wall so there is little chance of anyone not being able to see. Unfortunately, this may result in a distorted image, wider at the top than the bottom. This distortion is commonly referred to as keystoning. To overcome this keystoning effect we

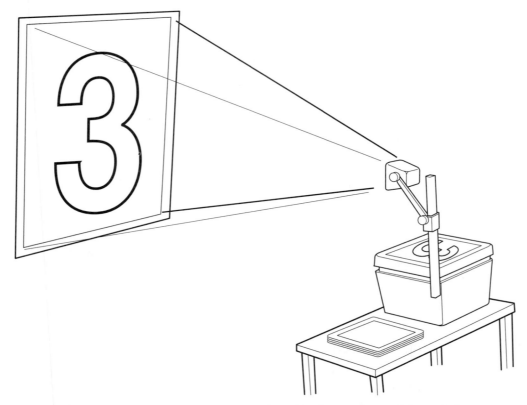

Make sure that none of your presentation aids obscure the participants' view

need to use an angled screen. The screen may be angled using wall brackets or if we are using a normal roll-up projection screen we can get attachments to make the screen tilt.

| Making transparencies

The blank transparencies are normally purchased separately or in boxes of one hundred. There are different colours, sizes and thicknesses. Check with your supplier to find out what will be best for your needs. The transparencies are also referred to by some people as acetates or foils.

The first thing we need to do when making an overhead transparency is to work out what information we want to project. When we first start out as presenters we have the temptation to include everything we possibly can on the transparency. Don't fall into this trap. An overhead transparency should only contain key words, phrases or diagrams. The most you want to put on

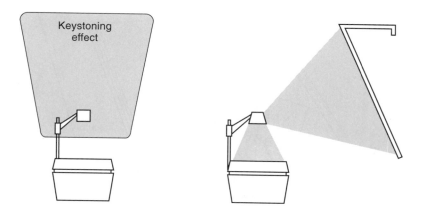

An overhead projector needs an angled screen if the image is being projected well above head level

a transparency would be five or six lines of writing with six or seven words in each line. This is not much, so make sure it is effective.

When we know what we want to put on our transparency, we need to lay it out so that it looks presentable. It's best to do a rough pen and paper layout so that we know what it should look like. When designing the layout, leave a 2–3 centimetre wide border around the edges. Now that we know what we want to include, and what the layout should look like, we can start on the final version.

Neat and clear presentation is an important part of any written or diagrammatic presentation material

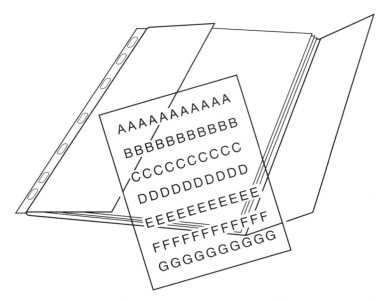

Commercially produced lettering systems are available for use on overhead projector transparencies

There are four basic ways of making the final transparency. The first way is to lay the transparency in front of us and draw what we want using either permanent or water-soluble overhead projection pens.

Make sure that your lettering is large enough and legible for all to see and read. When you first start producing overhead transparencies, allow for a couple of trial ones so that you can get the feel of it.

Using a permanent overhead projection pen means that what we put on the transparency is permanent. If we use water-soluble projection pens it allows us to erase any or all of the artwork easily. Each has its own advantages and disadvantages. If you do use water-soluble pens though, be aware that they wipe off easily. You may walk into a training session with blank transparencies as a result of paper rubbing on them. Both types of pen are available in a wide range of colours and thicknesses.

There are also a number of other lettering systems and machines available on the market. However, they are generally expensive and tend to be available only in large organisations that have big budgets.

The second common way of making overhead transparencies is to use a photocopier. This is an extremely fast method. Check to make sure that your photocopier will accept transparencies, otherwise it may not be so fast after all! Transparencies suitable for photocopiers will be noted on the box. Take your blank transparencies and place them in the paper carrier tray in place of the photocopier paper. Put your master on the copy screen and push the button. All going well you now have your final product. You can produce overhead transparencies of almost anything (including photographs and publications) using this method. It also allows for a cut, paste and copy production. If you have an enlarging facility on your machine you may like to make use of it.

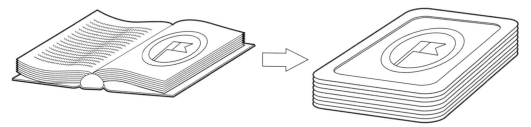

Photocopiers can often be used to create transparencies quickly and effectively

The only slight drawback with this method is that you are normally limited to black printing on your transparency (unless you are lucky enough to have a colour photocopier). To make your black and white transparency more interesting, or to highlight the really important points, you may wish to add a bit of colour by using overhead projection pens or by using colour-adhesive film.

You may see continuous rolls of transparency film being used occasionally. The roll is attached to the side of the overhead projector and wound across the projection screen. This type of presentation is not very common as it's extremely difficult to alter or update material and usually all of the artwork for the roll has to be done by hand.

The third way of producing overhead transparencies is with the use of a computer and printer. These are generally fast to produce and require a minimum amount of time to produce them. It is also relatively easy to produce colour overheads if you have access to a colour printer.

Always check your manuals for the production of transparencies. Printers and software packages vary in this matter. There are also some excellent dedicated software packages for these productions as well. Check with your computer suppliers for this.

The fourth way of producing overheads is to do them completely on computer using a dedicated program such as Microsoft PowerPoint, then use a display unit that fits on top of your overhead projector. The display unit has a clear screen in the centre of it that shows your 'page'. This acts as your transparency. These systems are now readily available and relatively easy to

Multimedia projector linked to a laptop computer

use. Their main advantage is that your transparencies can be modified at any time with a minimum of effort. The main disadvantage is that there are now more things to go wrong or break down.

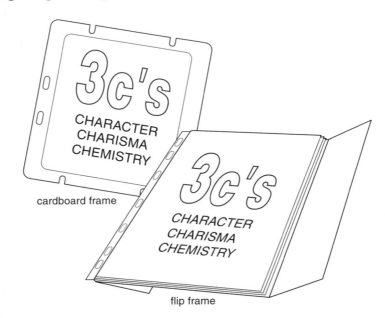

Different frames are available for use on transparencies and help to protect them from damage

After the standard single sheet transparency has been produced it may be mounted in a cardboard frame or a flip frame. With either of these methods we are able to write notes on the side of the frame.

One of the few problems with the cardboard frame is that it's too large to fit in most folders or in a brief case. The flip frame on the other hand is not much bigger than the transparency itself. It also has punched holes down one side for use in a ring folder. It can, therefore, be kept alongside with your session plans with everything in one place and in the correct sequence.

Let's now look at some more advanced types or designs of overhead transparencies.

Overlay method

Start with a base transparency and keep adding information to it by overlaying other transparencies on top. This is good to use to show how things are constructed or how things go together.

The overlay method allows the presenter to build up a total picture gradually

Write on as you use method

Use your original transparency as a starting point and build to it by writing additional information on it while you use it. This would be useful for showing how forms are filled in. Use a water-soluble pen so that you are able to reuse the transparency.

Write on the transparencies to add extra information as the session progresses

Disclosure methods

Using a disclosure method allows us to reveal certain sections of the overhead transparency as they are required. Methods vary from scrap pieces of paper to hinged pieces of board and can become quite involved.

A quick tip if you use a sheet of paper in the disclosure method. Place your masking sheet under the transparency. This allows you to see what is written without sliding the paper too far and perhaps giving more information than required.

Parts of the transparency can be disclosed gradually as the presenter moves to new information

Tips for using an overhead projector and transparencies

- Check the focus before the presentation starts.
- When placing the overhead transparency on the projector, place it the right way up so that you can read it while looking at the audience.
- Place the transparency squarely on the top plate.
- Ensure the projector is level so that the cooling fan operates at optimum level.
- Don't switch the projector off completely until the cooling fan stops.
- Keep eye contact with the audience, don't look at the screen.
- Turn the projector off when changing transparencies.
- Use a pointer on the transparency to show details.
- Mask sections of the transparency not required (revealing techniques).
- Turn the projector off when talking of something different to that being projected.
- Don't leave the projector turned on for extended periods.
- Have all of your transparencies in the correct order.
- Let the projector cool down before moving.
- Have a spare globe handy (some machines have spare globes built in and can be operated from a switch on the unit).
- Don't place your hands on the glass or lenses.
- Don't clean lenses with solvents, you may melt them. Use a soft tissue soaked in warm soapy water.
- Practise with the projector before using (some are slightly different from others).
- The projector can also be used to silhouette items, keys, etc.
- Use colours on your transparencies for greater interest.
- Keep transparencies simple and legible.
- Have the overhead projector serviced regularly.

Conclusion

The overhead projector is fast becoming a standard piece of equipment for the professional speaker. As all professional speakers become familiar with the overhead projector, only the best users will be remembered.

To be best, you will need to practise with the equipment until you feel as comfortable with it as you do with your best friend.

The new presenter has only to follow the information supplied here on the use of the overhead projector and on the production of overhead transparencies. With that as a base they will probably find that they know as much, if not more, than the professional public speaker now does. Proficiency indicates professionalism, so become proficient.

Practice and sound preparation will make you proficient in the use of the overhead projector

Further reading

Kalish, Karen, *How To Give A Terrific Presentation*, Amacom, New York, 1997.

CHAPTER 18

Using a microphone

A microphone used correctly can be a great bonus to someone giving a presentation to a large group of people. But one used badly can be a disaster.

Microphones are not difficult to use—all they require is a little understanding and some practice

A microphone is no guarantee of audibility. Think about the times you have spent standing at railway stations trying to understand what's being said through the dozens of speakers all linked together. Was that your train they just called or were they trying to find a missing child?

Faulty adjustment, weak batteries and poor use can make them squeal unbearably. They can also get knocked over and people can trip over the cables. The microphone that slides slowly down the stand forcing the speaker to bend over it ever lower and lower is well known to many comedians.

Most people have a fear of using microphones, but there's really no point in giving a presentation when only half of the people present can hear you.

When installed and used correctly, the microphone system can be a valuable resource for a speaker in a large room or hall trying to address a large group of people.

Make sure your microphone is adjusted properly before you begin your presentation

Microphones are not difficult to use. All they require is a little understanding and some practice.

There are three main types of microphones.

A **fixed** (or standard) microphone is on a stand or attached directly to a lectern. Occasionally these can be removed and held in the hand.

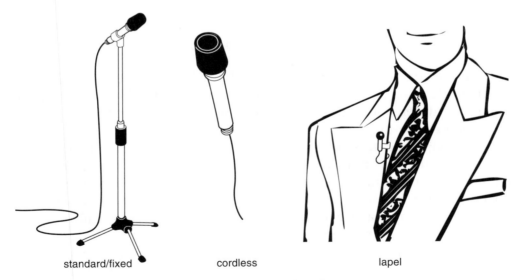

standard/fixed   cordless   lapel

The three types of microphones

A **cordless** microphone gives much more freedom of movement. It is held in the hand instead of being on a stand, and has no cable coming from it.

A **lapel** microphone is clipped to your lapel, tie, shirt or dress. It allows you full use of your hands. These are generally cordless.

You will need to choose a microphone to suit your own style. If you talk with your hands a lot you probably won't feel comfortable using a hand-held cordless unit. You would probably prefer to use a standard-type unit or a lapel microphone.

If you like to move around a lot while giving your presentations, a standard (or fixed) unit probably won't suit you. You would probably prefer to use a cordless hand-held unit or a lapel microphone. If possible, you need to experiment with each of them to see which suits your style best.

Regardless of which type of microphone you are using, make certain that you test it before starting your presentation if you can. Sometimes this will be someone else's responsibility and sometimes yours.

Testing is best done with someone helping you. Ask the other person to stand normally and talk into the microphone with his or her usual voice while you move around the room. What you need to do while walking around is to set the correct volume for the system, and select the best place for the microphone to be positioned, if it's fixed on a stand. Listen for any dead spots between speakers if there are two or more being used. Also listen for any feedback. Feedback is the squealing noise given when the microphone gets too close to the speaker (very distracting). After that has been done, swap positions with your helper and get them to check.

The position from your mouth of fixed microphones will vary but, as a general rule of thumb, the microphone should be somewhere between 10 centimetres and 50 centimetres from your mouth. You will have to experiment with this. The microphone should be just below your chin and pointed slightly upwards. If you are one of several speakers you probably won't have the chance of setting it up perfectly for yourself beforehand, so make sure you know how the microphone adjustments work so that you can alter the microphone to suit yourself as unobtrusively as possible.

When testing the microphone don't use the old 'testing, one, two, three' approach. Use the microphone as you would with your presentation, and actually start the presentation. Your assistant is then in a great position to tell whether he or she can hear you, and importantly understand what you're saying.

When installed and used correctly, microphones can be a valuable aid in a presentation

Tips for use:
- Handle microphones with care, they are delicate and expensive.
- Get there early to test it.
- Do not blow into the microphone or tap it to test if it's turned on. This can cause damage.
- When testing a microphone use your 'script' and speak exactly as you will later on.
- When using a fixed or standard-type microphone keep within its range while giving your presentation.
- With a fixed microphone have it adjusted to your correct height. Don't stretch or bend, have it adjusted properly. Find out how to do this before starting.
- Speak across the microphone, not directly into it. This will avoid the popping of 'p's' and the sizzling of 's's'.
- Microphones will pick up every noise, so be careful of what you might mutter to yourself, thinking nobody can hear you.
- Don't cough or clear your throat into a microphone. If using a fixed microphone, turn your head away from it. If using a lapel microphone, put your hand over the top of it.
- If you are using a lapel microphone, make sure you put it on well before you start.
- Ensure that it has a fresh battery. They don't last terribly long!
- With lapel microphones also ensure that they aren't muffled by your clothing, or rubbing against them.

- When using a lapel microphone make sure you take it off—before you go home!
- And very importantly, if you go to the toilet during a break in your presentation—turn the microphone off before you go!

Microphones are very sensitive instruments. They can create problems but are nonetheless an immeasurable valuable aid to presenters. Above all, it is an instrument that can facilitate your ability to impact on an audience in a memorable and dynamic way.

Further reading

I would suggest here that you simply read through the instruction book that came with your microphone. It should give you some valuable tips.

CHAPTER 19

Multiculturalism in presentations

Delivering presentations in a multicultural society is more than an interesting experience or change of pace. By dealing with people from other cultures it allows us to draw on new participant experiences. This can have the effect of not only making it more interesting for you, but more interesting for the other participants, particularly if the experiences are meaningful to the group as a whole.

Giving presentations in a multicultural society recognises the demographic composition of society and its diversity of cultures and languages.

Multicultural issues aren't something that can be ignored in your presentations. Most countries are now planning for increased numbers of overseas-born residents in their staff numbers and in their training rooms.

Most presenters and trainers will find that a very large percentage of their groups have been born overseas or come from different cultures. These percentages will continue to grow.

To assist new presenters when they are presenting to a group of mixed cultures, I have listed a few pointers to be followed.

Public speakers frequently find that many members of their groups are born overseas and/or are from different cultures

144

- Speak clearly and pause occasionally.
  Not 'Gizalookatyareport',
  but 'Can I have a look at your report?'
- Frequently check understanding, but avoid yes/no questions.
  Not 'Do you understand?',
  but 'How would you describe it?'
- Don't drop words when speaking, it doesn't help.
  Not 'Put here',
  but 'Put it here.'
- Avoid raising your voice, they are not deaf.
  Not yelling to get the message through,
  but speaking in a normal voice.
- Give notice when you are changing topics.
  Not just carrying on,
  but 'Now we've completed that, let's go on to ... '
- Don't use sarcastic remarks, they may be misunderstood.
  Not 'Sure it is' (said sarcastically),
  but 'I don't think that's right.'
- Use simple everyday words
  Not 'A philatelist',
  but 'A person who collects stamps.'
- Avoid complicated sentences or ideas.
  Not putting numerous ideas together,
  but presenting them one at a time.
- Give instructions in the sequence to be followed.
  Not 'Before you write it see me',
  but 'See me first then write it.'
- Try not to use strings of negatives.
  Not 'You can't do it if you haven't got one of these',
  but 'You need one of these to do it.'
- Use direct questions.
  Not 'You've done it haven't you?',
  but 'Have you done it yet?'
- Slang and colloquialisms will create confusion.
  Not 'Pull the other one',
  but 'Are you trying to trick me?'
- Be patient.
  Sometimes it takes a lot of time and understanding so you need to be patient.

While it's understood that there are different levels of understanding on the participant's part, I am aiming at a presentation situation where all of the participants are reasonably fluent in the presenter's language but may occasionally come across some stumbling blocks in communication or learning.

The list of pointers given above is also relevant for use with participants who speak your language but with a different accent. Sometimes it's assumed that a participant who speaks your language will understand you. Experienced travellers, public speakers and trainers will tell you, correctly, that this is not the case, and these situations may, in fact, be more of a problem than we are generally aware of.

Our participants' learning habits have been developed from their schooling and work experience. These habits will differ from culture to culture, from subculture to subculture and from individual to individual within the subcultures.

While it's easy to say that we should have a knowledge of these participants' learning habits, most of the time it is impractical. It is more practical to say that we should be aware of different learning habits and allow for them in the training room.

It's worth noting that in some languages we are faced with the additional problem of not having technical terms with equivalent meanings. This is something that an international public speaker or trainer must be aware of. However, in most typical public speaking situations the points covered previously will suffice.

If you are placed in a situation where an interpreter is required, make certain that they are a professional interpreter and not just someone who is bilingual. A bilingual translation may not get the correct message across.

If you're going to be presenting to groups with markedly different cultures or where your language may not be understood, it should be obvious that additional training on your part may be required.

Conclusion

As professional public speakers we must deal with a lot of different situations. The multicultural issues in presentations haven't been recognised for long, but it's now expected by our employers that we will be able to take control of these situations.

The other point here is that the participants can see us working effectively with these problems and may learn some of our skills by simple observation techniques. This has to be an added benefit to the presenter, the employee and the employer.

Further reading

Heerman, Barry, *Building Team Spirit*, McGraw-Hill Book Company, New York, 1997.

As I have mentioned, the issue of multiculturalism in public speaking and training is a new area of study. Research has shown that not a lot has been published about it.

Should you require further information on this topic you should contact the relevant government department in your area.

CHAPTER 20

Getting ready

Checklists are a handy tool for even the most experienced presenter

This chapter provides you with a number of checklists that may be appropriate for you as a public speaker. Most of the material being presented in this chapter is a summary of information that has already been presented in previous chapters. However, as there are so many things that a new presenter has to learn from experience, it is impossible to tie everything up in a neat parcel.

I would like to think that this book has assisted the new presenter and trainer in a number of ways, with these checklists adding to the support.

When you are given the task of completely organising a new presentation or training course, you will find that there are numerous jobs that have to be done. The following checklist has been compiled to make this task easier for you. It deals specifically with training issues but is also suited to general presentations.

```
┌─────────────────────────────────────────────────────────┐
│  OUTSIDE WORKSHOP CHECKLIST                               │
├─────────────────────────────────────────────────────────┤
│  COURSE TITLE: _____ │
│  COURSE DATES: _____ │
├─────────────────────────────────────────────────────────┤
│  Number of participants                                   │
│  Book venue                                               │
│  Request nominations                                      │
│  Invite speakers                                          │
│  Design topic list                                        │
│  Prepare session notes                                    │
│  Design program                                           │
│  Write fact sheet                                         │
│  Book/order equipment                                     │
│  Book/order materials                                     │
│  Prepare handouts                                         │
│  Handouts printed                                         │
│  Prepare presentation aids                                │
│  Prepare certificates                                     │
│  Book transport (speakers)                                │
│  Book transport (participants)                            │
│  Check nominations                                        │
│  Book accommodation                                       │
│  Advise supervisors                                       │
│  Confirm speakers                                         │
│  Confirm participants                                     │
│  Distribute fact sheet                                    │
│  Distribute pre-course materials                          │
│  Organise participants' needs                             │
│  Confirm accommodation                                    │
│  Purchase consumable items                                │
│  Organise coffee/tea, etc.                                │
│  Organise meals                                           │
│  Invitations to management                                │
│  Pick up films, videos, etc.                              │
│  Prepare name tags                                        │
│  Check stationery                                         │
│  Other _____                                       │
│  Other _____                                       │
│  Other _____                                       │
│  Other _____                                       │
│  Double check everything again                            │
└─────────────────────────────────────────────────────────┘
```

As with all of the material in this book, it has been designed to suit my needs; please treat it as a base to build your own checklists.

With so many items to check off it can become confusing to work out when certain things need to be done. You may find that this checklist is better if it's displayed in chart form as a task timeline. By transferring the information from your checklist to a task timeline you will avoid missing items.

Some of the items have been included from the previous checklist for the example below of a task timeline.

Task timeline										
Course title										
		← TIME → (to be done by)								
		19/1	30/1	12/2	25/2	30/2	15/3	21/3	25/3	28/3
	Establish numbers	← →								C
	Book venue	← →								R
	Request nominations		← →							I
S	Invite speakers		← →							S
E	Design topic list			← →						I
Q	Design program			← →						S
U	Write fact sheet			← →						
E	Book equipment				← →					
N	Book materials				← →					P
C	Prepare handouts				← →					O
E	Print handouts					← →				I
	Prepare aids				← →					N
	Prepare certificates						← →			T
	Book transport			← →						first
	....									day of
	.... etc									course

A task timeline helps you to prepare in an organised way to meet a deadline

Computer programs are available to help you organise your course diary. A critical path analysis can be worked out by entering the start date of the course and the date you want to start organising it. The rest of the information is worked out for you by the program. As these are complete packages, I don't feel that I need to give you any other information on them.

That takes care of the course prework. Now let's look at a checklist that will be of use to new trainers who think they are ready to present a session to a group.

SESSION CHECKLIST

SESSION TITLE: _____

SESSION DATES: _____

Are my session notes legible?	_____
Are my session objectives clear?	_____
Do I know who the group is?	_____
Do I have a motivator for the group?	_____
Am I building on previous knowledge?	_____
Is the session content the right size?	_____
Do I have the right number of points?	_____
Is the sequence of points logical?	_____
Are the presentation aids relevant?	_____
Are the handouts clear?	_____
Are the presentation aids appropriate?	_____
Are the presentation aids all operational?	_____
Is there plenty of participant activity?	_____
Have I planned to link forward?	_____
Have I included a session summary?	_____
Is my session evaluation suitable?	_____
Have I rehearsed my session?	_____
How many principles used? — R?	_____
— A?	_____
— M?	_____
— P?	_____
— 2?	_____
— F?	_____
— A?	_____
— M?	_____
— E?	_____

The day before the course may also require a bit of input from you.

THE DAY BEFORE CHECKLIST	
COURSE TITLE: _____	
COURSE DATES: _____	
Is the training room ready?	_____
Do I have extra markers, etc?	_____
Is the equipment set up?	_____
Is the seating arranged as required?	_____
Is all of my equipment ready?	_____
Can everyone see me and the equipment?	_____
Am I still familiar with the material?	_____
Do I know where all of the spares are?	_____

Next is a simple checklist for you to use before the session is due to start.

THE BEFORE YOU GO IN CHECKLIST	
COURSE TITLE: _____	
COURSE DATES: _____	
Get there early	_____
Recheck my equipment	_____
Set up my presentation aids	_____
Organise and place my notes	_____
Warm up my voice	_____
Mentally recall the sequence of events	_____
Breathe deeply	_____

Although the next checklist is titled 'During your presentation', it should be used shortly after you finish giving your session. By using it soon after the session you will be able to recall more of the points listed. Recognising that parts of your session may have been better can almost solve the problem.

DURING YOUR PRESENTATION CHECKLIST
COURSE TITLE: _____
COURSE DATES: _____

Do I avoid speaking softly?	_____
Did I avoid mumbling?	_____
Did I avoid speaking slowly?	_____
Did I avoid speaking too fast?	_____
Did I avoid a monotone presentation?	_____
Did I avoid pacing?	_____
Did I avoid frequent coughing?	_____
Did I avoid indecision?	_____
Did I avoid fiddling?	_____
Did I avoid other nervous habits?	_____
Did I avoid talking to the board?	_____
Was I well prepared?	_____
Was I animated?	_____
Was I enthusiastic?	_____
Did I summarise frequently?	_____
Was there two-way communication?	_____
Was my appearance suitable?	_____
Did I use all of the nine principles?	_____
Did my audience achieve the objectives?	_____

This next checklist will show you quickly whether or not your questioning techniques need to be improved.

QUESTION AND ANSWER CHECKLIST
COURSE TITLE: _____
COURSE DATES: _____
Do I encourage questions?   _____
Do I anticipate the correct questions?   _____
Do I practise the correct response?   _____
Do I use eye contact to involve the group?   _____
Do I repeat the question so it is heard?   _____
Do I repeat the question for clarification?   _____
Do I listen carefully?   _____
Do I allow other participants to answer?   _____

As communication plays a major part in our presentations and training sessions, a communication checklist has been included.

COMMUNICATION CHECKLIST
COURSE TITLE: _____
COURSE DATES: _____
Did I speak to the participants?   _____
Did the participants speak to me?   _____
Did the participants speak to each other?   _____

If we can place three ticks on this list we can safely say that there was three-way communication during the presentation or training session.

It's a good idea occasionally to have someone come and sit in on your session so that you can get some constructive feedback on your teaching techniques. Make sure that you tell the observer that you are after constructive feedback, otherwise you're likely to get a blank sheet of paper given back to you.

OBSERVER'S CHECKLIST	
COURSE TITLE: _____	
COURSE DATES: _____	
Were the main points emphasised?	_____
Was eye contact made?	_____
Was eye contact kept?	_____
Did the presenter stand upright?	_____
Was the presenter's position varied enough?	_____
Was the pitch varied?	_____
Was everything clearly spoken?	_____
Did the presenter read the audience?	_____
Were the objectives achieved?	_____

Any, or all, of the other checklists may be given to an observer so that your total performance may be assessed. After all, if you don't know about it how can you fix it?

When you present a session where you feel everything went well, you will probably find that you can tick most of the points given in the 'nerves' checklist. Alternatively, when you give a session where you feel extremely anxious you may find that very few of these points have been taken into consideration.

NERVES CHECKLIST	
COURSE TITLE: _____	
COURSE DATES: _____	
Did I breathe deeply?	_____
Did I mentally rehearse before going in?	_____
Did I arrive early?	_____
Did I look professional?	_____
Did I try to anticipate questions?	_____
Did I check all of my equipment?	_____
Did I establish my credibility?	_____
Did I use my session notes?	_____
Did I motivate the group?	_____
Did I move around?	_____
Did I practise my presentation?	_____
Did I know what I was talking about?	_____
Did I use the self-fulfilling prophecy?	_____

| Conclusion

The speaker needs to be aware of the many things that need to be prepared properly. All of these things tend to fall into one of the four categories shown below:

- presenter behavioural attitudes
- physical preparation
- mental preparation
- teaching and learning principles.

If a speaker is lacking in any of these areas, it's going to make it difficult to create a suitable learning atmosphere.

This book has attempted to cover as many of these areas as possible, but if you don't apply yourself to this information it can't work.

> There's never time
> to do it properly,
> but there's always time
> to do it over.

Further reading

As this chapter relates to the whole sphere of public speaking, training and psychology, I can't create a specific list of texts for your further reading.

Nearly every book that has been written about public speaking and training will have some kind of input to your 'getting ready'. Even texts and articles that are out of date can help you. When looking at things that have been tried previously you will probably find the results of their use. It will save you experiencing the same problems.

A final word

The previous twenty chapters will have given you more than enough theory to allow you to become a professional public speaker or trainer. However, theory alone is not enough. The time is now here for you to practise what you have read.

If you are new at public speaking or training or have little experience, the best way to spend your time now is practising and trying to improve your style. If you are fortunate enough to still have time available before you give your first presentation or commence your first program, use the time to study other professional speakers and trainers.

Experienced public speakers and trainers who happen to be thumbing through this book will certainly be given a few new ideas and have a lot of existing knowledge reinforced.

As there aren't many professional speakers and trainers in existence, I would request that those who do exist take responsibility for the coaching of the new, inexperienced or unprofessional speakers that they come into contact with. You will find that it's an incredible buzz to see one of your trainees giving a professional performance and you will know deep down that it's because of your time and their effort.

For the new speaker and trainer, happy presentation, and don't forget that your audience is the most important thing for you to consider.

Common terms

adviser   someone who has the responsibility of ensuring that the participants' learning is on the right path and is able to offer assistance when required.

aids   any form of presentation aid or thing that assists learning or teaching.

audiovisual aid   usually an electronic presentation aid that has pictures and/or sound.

brainstorming   a group method for gaining a lot of ideas or suggestions. Also refer to synergism.

buzz group   a small group of participants working on a task.

case study   a technique where the participants are given a situation to look at and are then required to solve problems or make decisions.

checklist   a list of relevant items that are either required or should be considered.

computer-based training   is any training that takes place on a computer and is under the direction of the program itself.

conference   a group of people who get together to exchange ideas on a specific topic.

course   generally refers to a group of people who are attending some form of presentation. It may also refer to the whole, or total, of the instruction.

DACUM   a process to develop a curriculum by breaking a job or position down into tasks.

delphi technique   a group technique for solving problems or dealing with specific situations that does not require the group to meet.

discovery learning   where learners learn by doing, rather than by relying heavily on the academics.

evaluation   generally to test and compare results.

exercise   generally refers to any structured experience the participants are involved in.

experiential learning   same as discovery learning.

facilitator   a presenter who lets the group become responsible for the learning outcome. A facilitator normally controls the group process rather than just teaching it.

feedback   is usually constructive information on the course material given to the participants or the presenter.

field trip   any trip to a location to observe something to do with the presentation.

fishbowl   a group process using a discussion group and an observer group.

159

flip chart   an easel with large sheets of paper.

games   normally a discovery exercise where participants learn by experience. Games usually have rules and are competitive.

icebreaker   a quick game or exercise designed to get participants settled and/or mixing with each other.

instructor   the person who instructs, trains, teaches or informs an individual or a group of people.

learner-centred training   a training situation where participants take responsibility for their learning.

lecture   a one-way communication from the lecturer to the group lesson. See session.

multicultural   mixed races, nationalities or cultures.

needs analysis   the method of determining a training need.

networking   getting to know other participants. May be used to support or assist each other during or after the instruction.

nominal group process   a structured problem-solving process that doesn't require participants to interact to start with.

objective   a statement giving the goals to be achieved.

observer   someone who watches a group process and gives feedback on it.

OHP   abbreviation of overhead projector.

OHT   abbreviation of overhead transparency.

organisational development   planned training or development of staff to meet planned organisational goals.

outdoor training   is any training or activity that takes place outdoors.

overhead projector   electronic projector that projects overhead transparency images onto a wall or screen.

overhead transparency   sheet of transparent film with information written or drawn on. Used with overhead projectors.

participant   someone who is attending a training program or is involved in any group process.

presentation aid   anything that assists in the delivery of your presentation.

presenter   the person who gives a presentation to an individual or group of people.

prework   anything the participant has to do as advance work for a course.

program   see course.

recognition of prior learning   is giving someone credit for previously gained knowledge or previously gained skills. This prior learning may be done either formally or informally.

recorder   someone who is given the task of writing down key points or ideas generated by a group.

reinforcement   encouragement or praise given to a participant to keep their interest or increase their motivation.

role-play   normally participants are given specific roles to act out in front of, or with, the group.

RPL   abbreviation of recognition of prior learning.

seminar   an information session or problem-solving session where the participants have the same need or problem identified.

session   any single presentation that deals with one specific topic. It may last from a few minutes to several days.

simulation   an exercise designed to create a real-life atmosphere.

student   see participant.

synergism   when a group of people get together to generate ideas, they generate more (and better) ideas than the total of the ideas that may have been generated individually.

T-group   normally an unstructured program where individuals find out how their behaviour affects others and vice versa.

team building   a training program designed to make a group of people work together as a team.

test   a way of determining a participant's level of knowledge, skill expertise or behaviour in a given area.

trainee   see participant.

trainer   the person who trains, instructs, teaches or informs an individual or a group of people.

training aid   something that assists in the delivery of your training.

training gap   see training need.

training need   the difference between what an employee can do now and what they are required to do in order to carry out their job effectively and efficiently.

video   can be used to describe a video camera and recorder, video player or video cassette tape.

whiteboard   smooth white-surfaced board that can be written on with special whiteboard markers.

workshop   a participative training program where the participants learn by doing.

Bibliography

The literature in public speaking and human relations training and their closely related fields is growing rapidly. The speaker or trainer who wishes to advance in this area is urged to study the concepts of training and development to their limit. This book is the starting point, this bibliography is the next step.

The publications that have been marked with an asterisk should be in all public speakers' and trainers' permanent libraries as you will find that you will be referring to them on a constant basis.

Baird, L., Schneier, C. & Laird, D., *The Training and Development Sourcebook*, 2nd edn, Human Resource Press, Massachusetts, 1994. ⋆

Bishop, Sue, *Training Games for Assertiveness and Conflict Resolution*, McGraw-Hill Book Company, New York, 1997.

Blanchard, Kenneth & Johnson, Spencer, *The One Minute Manager*, William Collins, Great Britain, 1983. ⋆

Boydell, T. H., *A Guide to the Identification of Training Needs*, 2nd edn, British Association for the Commercial and Industrial Education, London, 1983.

Brown, J., Lewis, R. & Harcleroad, F., *AV Instruction Technology, Media and Methods*, 6th edn, McGraw-Hill Book Company, New York, 1983.

Burnard, Philip, *Training Games for Interpersonal Skills*, McGraw-Hill Book Company, New York, 1994.

Cohen, L. & Manion, L., *Research Methods in Education*, 4th edn, Croom Helm, London, 1994.

Craig, Robert, *Training and Development Handbook*, 4th edn, McGraw-Hill Book Company, New York, 1996. ⋆

Daniels, William, *Group Power: A Manager's Guide to Using Meetings*, University Associates, California, 1986.

Donaldson, Les & Scannell, Edward, *Human Resource Development: The New Trainer's Guide*, 2nd edn, Addison-Wesley Publishing Company, Massachusetts, 1986.

Eitington, Julius, *The Winning Trainer*, 3rd edn, Gulf Publishing Company, Houston, 1996. ⋆

Elgood, Chris, *Handbook of Management Games*, 5th edn, Gower Publishing Company, England, 1993.

Field, Laurie, *Skilling Australia*, Longman Cheshire, Melbourne, 1990. ⋆

Forbess-Greene, Sue, *The Encyclopedia of Icebreakers*, University Associates, California, 1983.

Gronlund, Norman, *Stating Objectives for Classroom Instruction*, 3rd edn, Macmillan Publishing, New York, 1985.

Heermann, Barry, *Building Team Spirit*, McGraw-Hill Book Company, New York, 1997.

Honey, Peter, *The Trainer's Questionnaire Kit*, McGraw-Hill Book Company, New York, 1997.

Howes, Virgil, *Individualization of Instruction*, Macmillan Publishing, New York, 1970.

Hughes, Shirley, *Professional Presentations*, McGraw-Hill Book Company, Sydney, 1990.

Kalish, Karen, *How To Give A Terrific Presentation*, Amacon, New York, 1997.

Kirk, James & Kirk, Lynne, *Training Games for the Learning Organisation*, McGraw-Hill Book Company, New York, 1997.

Knowles, Malcolm, *Self-Directed Learning*, Cambridge, New York, 1975.

Knowles, Malcolm, *The Adult Learner: A Neglected Species*, 4th edn, Gulf Publishing Company, Houston, 1995. ⋆

Knowles, Malcolm, *Using Learning Contracts*, Jossey-Bass Publishers, California, 1986.

Kroehnert, Gary, *100 Training Games*, McGraw-Hill Book Company, Sydney, 1994. ⋆

Kroehnert, Gary, *Basic Training for Trainers*, 2nd edn, McGraw-Hill Book Company, Sydney, 1995. ⋆

Laird, Dugan, *Approaches to Training and Development*, 2nd edn, Addison-Wesley Publishing Company, Massachusetts, 1985. ⋆

Mager, Robert, *Developing Attitudes Toward Learning*, 2nd edn, David S. Lake Publishers, California, 1984.

Mager, Robert, *Measuring Instructional Results*, 2nd edn, Pitman Learning Company, California, 1984.

Mager, Robert, *Preparing Instructional Objectives*, 2nd edn, Pitman Learning Company, California, 1984. ⋆

Mager, Robert & Pipe, Peter, *Analysing Performance Problems*, 2nd edn, David S. Lake Publishers, California, 1984.

Mill, Cyril, *Activities for Trainers: 50 Useful Designs*, University Associates California, 1980.

Newstrom, J. W. & Scannell, E. E., *Games Trainers Play*, McGraw-Hill Book Company, New York, 1980.

Owens, Robert, *Organisational Behaviour in Education*, 5th edn, Prentice-Hall International, New Jersey, 1994.

Pagano, Robert, *Understanding Statistics in the Behavioral Sciences*, 4th edn, West Publishing, Minnesota, 1994.

Pease, Allan, *Body Language*, Camel Publishing Company, Sydney, 1981.

Pennington, F. C., *Assessing Educational Needs of Adults*, *New Directions for Continuing Education Quarterly Sourcebooks*, Jossey-Bass, San Francisco, 1980, Series No. 7.

Poulter, Bruce, *Training and Development*, CCH Australia Limited, Sydney, 1982.

Rae, Leslie, *How to Measure Training Effectiveness*, 3rd edn, Gower Publishing Company, England, 1996.

Rogers, Jennifer, *Adults Learning*, 2nd edn, Open University Press, England, 1979.

Romig, Dennis A., *Breakthrough Teamwork*, Irwin Professional Publishing, Chicago, 1996.

Scannell, E. E. & Newstrom, J. W., *More Games Trainers Play*, McGraw-Hill Book Company, New York, 1983.

Tindall, K., Collins, B. & Reid, D., *The Electronic Classroom*, McGraw-Hill Book Company, Sydney, 1973.

Turner, David, *60 Role Plays for Management and Supervisory Training*, McGraw-Hill Book Company, New York, 1996.

Video, *You'll Soon Get The Hang Of It*, Video Arts. ⋆

Video, *Right First Time*, NSW TAFE.

Zemke, R. & Kramlinger, T., *Figuring Things Out: A Trainers Guide to Needs and Task Analysis*, Addison-Wesley Publishing Company, Massachusetts, 1981.

Index

In-house training services

If you would like information on our in-house training services, please complete the information below and forward it on to us by mail or fax.

Name: _____

Title: _____

Organisation: _____

Address: _____

_____

_____

Phone: _____

Fax: _____

I would like further information on:

In-house presentation techniques courses ☐

In-house training techniques courses ☐

In-house time management courses ☐

In-house courses for other subjects ☐

_____

_____

_____

_____

_____

_____

Post to: Gary Kroehnert
Training Excellence
PO Box 169
Grose Vale NSW 2753
Or fax: (02) 4572 2200

Readers' comments and suggestions

If you would like to comment on any of the things written (or not written) about in this book, now is your time to do it. I would also appreciate suggestions and comments on the layout, wording or anything else you feel needs comment.

Gary Kroehnert

Suggestions for improvements

_____

_____

_____

_____

_____

_____

Additional comments

_____

_____

_____

_____

_____

_____

Please cut this form out and return to Product Manager, Professional and Reference, PPE, McGraw-Hill Book Company Australia Pty Limited, 4 Barcoo Street, East Roseville, NSW 2069.